THE WALKABLE CITY

The Walkable City

FROM HAUSSMANN'S BOULEVARDS TO
JANE JACOBS' STREETS AND BEYOND

Mary Soderstrom

Véhicule Press

Published with the generous assistance of the Canada Council for the Arts, the Book Publishing Industry Development Program of the Department of Canadian Heritage, and the Société de développement des entreprises culturelles du Québec (SODEC).

Cover design: David Drummond
Set in Adobe Minion by Simon Garamond
Printed by Marquis Printing Inc.

LIBRARY AND ARCHIVES CANADA CATALOGUING IN PUBLICATION

Soderstrom, Mary, 1942-

The walkable city : from Haussmann's boulevards to Jane
Jacobs' streets and beyond / Mary Soderstrom.
Includes bibliographical references.

ISBN 978-1-55065-243-7

1. Streets—Design. 2. City planning. 3. Pedestrian areas.

I. Title.

NA9053.S7S67 2008   711'.4   C2008-905777-5

Published by Véhicule Press, Montréal, Québec, Canada
www.vehiculepress.com

Distribution: LitDistCo
orders@litdistco.ca

Printed in Canada on 100% post-consumer recycled paper.

For

Sophie Bousquet
Emmanuel Nivon
Elin Soderstrom
Lukas Soderstrom

May they walk through life with joy

Contents

ONE

Starting Out in Search
of the Walkable City

CHAPTER 1

Looking for a House
A Sort-of Introduction

MANY YEARS AGO, when my husband and I found ourselves with a brand-new baby and an eviction notice from landlords who wanted our apartment for themselves, I spent a month in the dead of winter looking at houses. Our first choice would have been to rent again, but that year rental vacancies hit an all-time low. Since we'd succeeded in saving a little money—nothing like impending parenthood to sober up a young couple—we decided somewhat reluctantly that we ought to buy. Of course that made the whole exercise of looking for a place to live more stressful. Until then we'd thought of ourselves as free spirits, ready to take off on two weeks' notice if we wanted to. Suddenly we were being forced to make a decision that we'd have to live with for a number of years. It was a sleepless period, and not only because the baby wasn't yet sleeping through the night. The questions seemed endless. How big a house? What neighborhood? A duplex with a rental unit to make the financial burden lighter? Single family detached? A row house?

The only thing clear from the start was that we were going to live within walking distance of my husband's work. He is an energetic man who hates driving in traffic and riding on crowded public transportation. If he were forced to put up with the daily struggles and irritation of commuting by any means other than his own two feet, I was afraid he'd shuffle off this mortal coil before he hit forty-five.

Luckily, Montreal has several pleasant neighborhoods that are within walking distance of the central core. The house we bought is thirty-five minutes on foot from his office. The location came with other advantages: shopping streets two blocks away, schools not much further, and parks close enough for a toddler to walk to easily. In time I began to wonder why everybody didn't want to live in such a neighborhood. After my last book, *Green City: People, Nature and Urban Places* (2006, Véhicule Press), I began to think about the walkable city, its decline and its possible rebirth, particularly as a solution to the Green Paradox we currently are living, where the desire to claim a bit of nature for our own leads to urban sprawl.

I discovered that the idea that a city might not be walkable would never have occurred to anyone who lived before 1800. Walking was the way everyone but a few gentry and soldiers got around. With remarkable consistency, cities grew no larger than someone on foot could cross in an hour. And, with very few exceptions, paths, roads and streets just happened, as people went from one place to another, avoiding a big tree or following the contours of a hill. It took the might of an empire to build straight, paved roads. The Romans were the champions, because unless a powerful government wants to move infantry frequently and far, or depends on oxen to haul wagons, traffic moves quite well, thank you very much, on more modest roads.

The Industrial Revolution changed that, as it changed so many other things. The harnessing of steam power meant that people and goods could travel faster than was ever dreamed possible, that city streets, once perfectly capable of handling both foot and wagon traffic, became so crowded that movement was nearly impossible and that living conditions for ordinary people went from bearable to absolutely deplorable. Reaction, when it finally came, was built around three partial solutions: build better roads, clear away bad housing, and move as many people as possible to the suburbs. Along the way, the idea that people could get around in cities on their own muscle power was nearly forgotten. In the past century, the private automobile has pushed walkability further into the background.

Why does that matter? Who cares, really? We've got our cars and our patch of green outside the center of the city; we're pretty well set, aren't we? Perhaps—as long as we don't put much value on the time we spend commuting, on what we're doing to our planet as we guzzle petroleum products, or on the kind of social interaction and convenience that living where walking reigns can bring. Abandoned suburbs and social unrest are just two of the apocalyptic scenarios proposed for our future as the oil runs out, and we are already waging wars over petroleum

Baron Georges-Eugène Haussmann c. 1853, about the time
Napoléon III summoned him to Paris to remake the city.

Jane Jacobs: writer, urbanist, critic, woman of contradictions.
Photograph by Maggie Steber.

resources. What we're doing to our health is only slightly less disturbing: the jury is still out on just what is causing the marked increase in obesity observed around the developed world, but most health professionals agree that a sedentary, car-anchored lifestyle contributes greatly.

How did we start down this road? Is there any exit from this highway along which we're racing toward social and environmental crisis? Baron Georges-Eugène Haussmann, whose name is synonymous with the magnificent nineteenth-century reconstruction of Paris, can shed light on how our trip began. Jane Jacobs, the twentieth-century independent thinker, grappled with large questions of urban life, and spoke frequently about ways out of the cul-de-sacs we have constructed for ourselves. Together, their words, taken from their writings and interviews, may help us make sense of things. Their ideas suggest detours and new avenues that will get us past this bad patch and onto a roadway where we can walk together toward the future.

Admittedly, the two make a rather odd couple. One, the Baron Haussmann, was a well-connected administrator who is given the credit for transforming Paris into a city of broad boulevards and grand views. He was to be the inspiration of a hundred and fifty years of major projects around the world. He ruthlessly tore down whole neighborhoods and then reconstructed them, with the very best of intentions. With the hearty concurrence of Napoléon III, he spent millions of francs on his projects. Trained as a lawyer, he understood finance and appreciated the technical talents of engineers. His philosophy and plans had effects far beyond his city and his corner of Europe. He was a man of dignity and charm. And yes, most definitely a man, because no woman of his time worked unless she were royal like Queen Victoria, or poor, like the heroines of Émile Zola's muckraking novels.

The other, Jane Jacobs, was definitely a woman—Robert Moses, the authoritarian New York planner, once called her just one of a "bunch of mothers"—and her professional credentials were unorthodox. She had no university degree, but she began writing about architecture and urban affairs as a young woman. Her book *The Death and Life of Great American Cities* rattled cages when it was published in 1961, while her political action and later writings earned her great respect among urban planners and city-dwellers all over North America.

It is a delight to imagine them meeting on a brilliant spring day in the center of Paris, or sitting on Jane Jacobs' shady front porch on Albany Street in Toronto discussing their common passions for cities and their organization. The Baron could tell Ms. Jacobs how he remade an already great city into one that has captured the imagination of the world. His Paris, after all, is the city that German Generalleutnant Dietrich von Choltitz refused to burn even though Hitler commanded its destruction. It is the city that stood for romance, music, gaiety, beauty, and freedom when Humphrey Bogart bade goodbye to Ingrid Berman in *Casablanca*. "We'll always have Paris," Bogart said, and so we do, as an example of a lovely, walkable city almost in spite of itself.

Jane Jacobs would probably take the Baron to task for the way he ignored the fates of the thousands his reconstruction schemes displaced. She was always suspicious of grand projects; she had a very critical eye when it came to assessing ambitious plans made by powerful men aimed at reorganizing the world for others. But she surely would make a favorable comment or two about the lively street life of the city he left behind.

The Baron and Ms. Jacobs of course never met, but this book will propose walks that they might be interested in taking, had they the chance, walks in Paris, New York and Toronto, as well as other urban areas. Each walk is chosen because it tells something important about how we have organized the world and our cities, and each, it's hoped, will give a taste of a city at a particular point in its history.

What we will find at the end of the walking will not be a place where we can rest on high ground from which to survey with pleasure where we have come from, however. We may well find ourselves with some grand views, but we may look out on imminent destruction, directly linked to the way we have left the walkable city behind. Courage, though. The longest journey begins with the first step. Let us start by looking at what walking, itself, is.

[CHAPTER 2]

These Feet Were Made for Walking
How It All Began

WAIST-HIGH GRASS rustles as we walk single-file along the path worn down by many feet. Look around: in the far distance mauve shadows of hills mark the horizon, fading to blue-gray on the far edges of our line of sight. Darker, dusty green shadows indicate where a tree or two might be growing on the edge of a watercourse which has cut its way through the savannah or where water has welled up in a spring. The wind rushes across the plain, laying down a background murmur which sets the scene for this most human adventure, a walk across a savannah. The grassland might be in East Africa, or it could be on the plains and steppes of central and eastern Europe, the vast center of North America, or the outback of Australia. The rains have brushed the landscape with green at this moment, and so it is particularly satisfying to the human eye and augurs well for hunting.

This is the kind of landscape on which humans evolved over hundreds of thousands, if not millions, of years, where we stood up on our hind legs and began to walk upright all the time. The consequences have been enormous.

Walking can be seen as the quintessential human activity, the literal and figurative step which led to everything we are today. The traits that brought success in that landscape are still with us, and while we can work around them, we ignore them at our peril. To better understand them, it helps to look at our nearest cousins, the chimpanzees.

There he is, sitting relaxed, looking calmly off to his left as if waiting for a friend. One arm lies on the branch in front of him, while the other rests on his knee. His fingers and his palm are long, but it is clear that these hands are made to grasp objects easily. The thumb can swivel around to oppose the fingers. Together they are able to manipulate things as thin as a long stem of grass or as bulky as a stone that might be covering an anthill. True, his hands are covered in dark fur, but their range of movement and delicacy of touch are not impossibly different from our own.

But it is not the chimpanzee's hands that tell the tale. Look rather at the chimp's feet in this illustration from Alfred Russel Wallace's 1871 treatise on natural selection, *Darwinism: An Exposition on the Theory of Natural Selection with Some of Its Applications*. There you'll see just what a long road humans—the world's champion two-legged walkers—have traveled.

We know now that chimps share something like 98 percent of their genetic coding with us, but, long before the principles of inheritance were ever suspected, Wallace noted that the foot of an ape "is formed almost exactly like our hand." (Gregor Mendel's work on inheritance was well underway when Wallace wrote, but when Mendel died, ten years after Wallace's book was published, the importance of what Mendel had been doing was unknown. It wouldn't be until the beginning of the twentieth century that his work would be recognized, and nearly another hundred years before the building blocks of inheritance were uncovered.)

Wallace noted that the chimp's big toe looks and functions very much like the human thumb, which means that its feet grasp branches as efficiently as its hands can. The adaptive advantage of this is pretty obvious for creatures who spend most of their time in forested country: chimps are able to scamper easily up trees and swing from branch to branch. When they walk on the ground, it is most often on all fours, and, as Wallace observed, the soles of their feet "cannot be placed horizontally on the ground." Rather, a chimp walks on the outer edge of the foot with the toes partly closed. It leans forward so that its knuckles bear its weight in front. It can stand up. It can even walk short distances upright carrying things in both hands. At least one study also shows that this way of walking can be pretty energy-efficient, but chimps move a lot faster on four feet than on two.

Humans are quite different. A few may indulge in a little knuckle-walking. Football forwards when they get ready for the kick-off are the best example, but once the ball is snapped back, the forwards are up on two legs, ready to run.

Not that a football player's speed is as good as that of fleet-footed mammals who run on four legs: the fastest human sprinters have been clocked at only 10.2 meters (32.7 feet) per second for less than 15 seconds—the current 100-meter sprint record is 9.69 seconds. But mammals who specialize in running, be they predators like cheetahs, prey like pronghorn antelopes, or domesticated animals bred for speed like horses and greyhounds, can gallop at a rate of 15 to 20 meters (49.2 to 65.7 feet) per second for several minutes. When humans run we burn up a lot more energy than do our fleet four-footed friends; it takes at least twice as much metabolic energy per distance traveled for us as for a horse, for example.

On the other hand, there is no doubt that the football player, like all normal humans, is far better on two legs than any animal. Dancing bears, gamboling monkeys, charging gorillas, and even some dogs with their eyes on a piece of kibble as a reward will walk upright. Kangaroos and birds may hop along, and it appears from reconstruction of fossils and fossilized footprints that some dinosaurs regularly put one back foot down and then the other. But Barney and other dinosaurs used their pelvises as fulcrums, balancing their weight front and back between torso and tail in a kind of teeter-totter. As Samuel Johnson notoriously said about preaching women, when other animals walk on their hind legs it's notable not necessarily because they're good at it, but because they do it all.

We are different indeed. No other animal has our peculiar arrangement of legs right below the body's center of gravity and a head perched directly on top of the spinal cord. The human spine is attached under the back of the skull at the foramen magnum. When paleontologists find a fossil bone with this sort of placement, they know that they're dealing with a creature who spent most of his or her life on two legs, upright. Furthermore, the spine which emerges from this hole curves first backward and then forward in a way unlike that of any other animal. The vertebrae of our lower back are much sturdier than those of our ape relatives because they must bear all the weight of the torso: in the other apes, the shoulders also bear weight when our cousins amble along on four limbs. As a result of our legs being attached where they are, our pelvises have been transformed into shallow cones from which our big-headed babies frequently have trouble escaping during birth.

And our feet. Our feet! No other animal has hind feet so elegantly differentiated from front feet, so clearly evolved to give us advantages in specific landscapes. As Leonardo da Vinci said, the human foot is a masterpiece of engineering and a work of art.

The fact that our bodies are engineered for upright walking is important in understanding our evolution, but of equal, if less understood, importance is the way our brains are programmed for it too. Hold a two-month-old baby with your hands under her arms and let her feet touch the ground. She'll step high with first one foot and the other, just as she'll fling her arms out from her body when she hears a loud noise and then slowly bring them back together as if ready to wrap them around her mother—or a branch. These automatic movements are from the kit of instinctive reflexes every normal child is born with. Vestiges of the startle, or Moro, reflex will accompany us all our lives, clicking in instantaneously so that we jump whenever we hear the sound

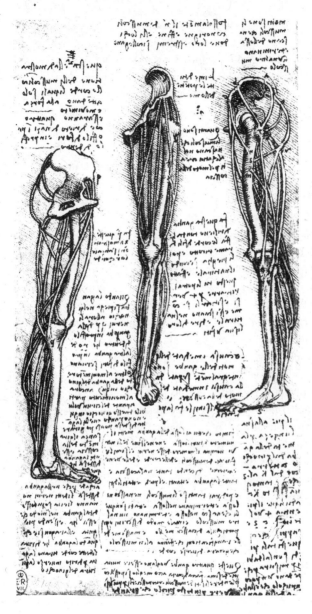

As Leonardo da Vinci said, the human foot is a masterpiece of engineering and a work of art.

of a crash outside or a lion's roar in the tall grass behind us. In normal babies, the stepping reflex will disappear for reasons which aren't clear, but a few months after it does most babies will crawl and then walk.

A very few people seem not to be programmed to walk upright at all, however. One inbred family in Turkey has five brothers and sisters out of nineteen who have never learned. They can stand, but their heads are pointed downwards, and they can only look in front of themselves with difficulty. To get around they lean forward with back legs flexed and arms extended, the palms of their hands hitting the ground the way the soles of their feet do. Uner Tan, the Turkish physician who first wrote about them, in *Neuroscience* in 2006, said that although their hands are calloused and rough, they can do a number of delicate things with them: the women crochet and knit, for example. They show considerable mental retardation, and speak a "language that only their parents and other siblings can understand."

Dr. Tan's findings note some genetic anomalies on Chromosome 17, but it is unlikely that one mutation is responsible for the constellation of behaviors that has resulted in us walking upright. It's notable that this family does not knuckle-walk like the other primates. They place their palms flat the way normal babies position their hands when they crawl, although babies usually use their knees for propulsion, while these people push off with their feet as they lean forward on their palms.

Bipedal locomotion is not without its downsides: our backaches and arthritic knees and hips can all be attributed to the twists and turns our bodies must make to walk upright. Obviously, though, walking on two feet gave us the opportunity to develop other tools we needed to survive, and to keep on walking.

Anthropologists generally agree that modern humans made their way out of Africa and into the Middle East about fifty thousand years ago. There is evidence that some of us may have hopscotched our way around the Indian Ocean, going from island to island and arriving very early in the New Guinea archipelago and the islands around Australia. This presented enormous intellectual and physical challenges, requiring, among other things, knowing how to make boats. Even though sea levels may have been low enough during the various Ice Ages that many land masses were linked, gaps remained that could only have been crossed by rafts or canoes.

Our ancestors who walked out of Africa were no less savvy and certainly carried with them a tool kit of some sophistication, including knives, axes, textiles, weapons, and baskets. What they wore on their feet, if anything, is open to question. In warm climates, walking over well-worn paths, even when the surface is rocky, presents few problems to people whose feet have had enough exposure to toughen the soles. (YouTube is full of videos of people walking barefoot over burning coals, broken glass, and sharp rocks, if you have any doubt.) But just as the shorter days during the winters in northern latitudes favored people who could produce more vitamin D because of their light skins, so the cold of snow and ice encouraged people to find ways to cover their feet. Examination of fossil feet suggests that people were wearing sturdy shoes as early as forty thousand years ago. Erik Trinkaus, anthropology professor at Washington University in St. Louis, Missouri, says that bones from that time show little toes which were weaker than the strength of leg bones would predict. Because our outside toes move much more when we walk barefoot than they do when feet are in shoes, this characteristic of early fossils speaks of feet well protected by some sort of covering. Trinkaus thinks that people may have begun wrapping their feet with skins or other insulating material even earlier. Weakened little toes are clear evidence of systematic foot protection. The oldest foot coverings still extant are quite a bit younger because the hides and plant material people used to make shoes don't endure, whereas bones fossilize. Nevertheless, the University of Oregon has a collection of sandals that are up to 10,500 years old. The oldest, a sage bark brush fiber model for an adult found in a central Oregon cave, has a hollow worn where its owner's big toe rubbed, while a somewhat younger sandal is pockmarked where sparks from a hearth fire singed the fiber. Other evidence of boots made for walking comes from the mummified man found in a melting glacier in the Alps in 1991. He died somewhere around 5,300 years ago, probably murdered. On his well-preserved feet were shoes with bearskin soles, stuffed with grass to make them warmer.

Examples of foot coverings that ordinary folk wore more recently are relatively rare. The fancy, elaborate shoes and boots of the rich and locally famous are more likely to have survived, if only because the best ones were used only for special occasions and so got less wear. Indeed, some of the most fascinating shoes from the past seem very hard to walk in, like those of an Egyptian Pharaoh with long toe-pieces that arch upward, or the high platforms of Venetian courtiers. Some shoes were not made for walking at all: elaborately decorated Sioux moccasins had soles covered with beaded floral designs that would be destroyed were they walked on. The moccasins were designed to be worn on horseback; the beadwork could be seen by those on the ground, underscoring the message, if you are on foot, you're not as important as I am, on horseback. The modern equivalents are the expensive delicate high-heeled shoes that fashionable women wear even though it's nearly impossible to walk more than a few steps in them. Not surprisingly, ugly, wide-toed, comfortable shoes are called "sensible" because wearing anything else to walk a distance makes no sense.

Whether one wore shoes or not, walking was the only way nearly everyone got around until practically yesterday in the long history of humans. Horses and draft animals were domesticated five or six thousand years ago, but only warriors and gentry used the former, and the latter's strength was needed to plow or haul loads, so speed was not as important as power. This meant that perhaps 95 percent of humanity born before the early nineteenth century never moved faster than a walk except when they broke into a run, and it wasn't until the 1820s that trains could go faster than the fastest runner. The current marathon record, held by Ethiopian Haile Gebrselassie, works out to around 22 kilometers (13.7 miles) an hour, a speed which steam locomotives didn't surpass until the Rainhill Trials in 1829.

Ordinary life was organized around the fact that an adult in reasonable physical shape can keep a steady pace of a little under five kilometers (around three miles) an hour for long distances. Some human walking feats appear truly astounding today. Several times during the great period of North American westward migration in the middle of the nineteenth century men and women pushing handcarts beat horse- or ox-drawn wagons crossing the prairie from the Missouri River to Salt Lake City. Eight companies of Mormon emigrants made the trek in eighty-one to a hundred and twenty-five days, averaging between 25 to 30 miles (40 to 48 kilometers) a day, compared to the 10 to 15 miles (16 to 24 kilometers) a day that wagons averaged.

On a day-to-day basis, people in the past regularly walked long distances. Geographer Richard Harris says that workers frequently lived up to an hour's walk from their workplace, which is about the limit that a man could go on foot and still put in a ten- or eleven-hour day. One study has also documented that young men in rural England frequently walked a couple of hours each way on Sunday to spend their one day off courting the girls of neighboring villages.

Today, however, it has become less and less common—some would say, less and less easy, also—for people to walk very much. Only 16 percent of American children walk or bike to school, for example, although as recently as the 1960s, more than 43 percent did just that. Legions of adults huff and puff when asked to go more than a block. The reasons for this big change in behavior are many, including the availability of faster means of transportation. But until the prosperity of the post-World War II period, even people relying on faster-than-walk transport to go considerable distances also did a fair amount of walking, getting from their homes to the train or trolley embarkation point, running errands, and visiting friends and relatives. That is no longer the case, and today's North American cities seem to have been built to make walking difficult. This may be having drastic effects on our health, just as the concomitant reliance on petroleum-fueled transport is having disastrous effects on our planet. Suffice to say for the moment, that simply because Americans are heavier now than they were forty years ago they use 938 million gallons (3,550 million liters) more gasoline annually than they would have in 1960 going the same distances.

But now let us allow the Baron to show us Paris, and what he did to it.

Two

Walking the Walk

Baron Georges-Eugène Haussmann and Napoléon III created modern Paris,
replacing winding medieval streets with broad boulevards.

CHAPTER 3

The Baron's Paris

THE GRASS in the Jardin des Tuileries on an imaginary spring Sunday early in the twenty-first century is not long and whispering the way grass is on a savannah. It is close-cropped and nicely disciplined into green lawns, offering relief to the eyes from the sunlight bouncing off the white gravel of the paths. The chairs set here and there along the length of the grand promenade are nearly full, with people of all ages, reading, talking, whispering, or—eyes closed, head back, face turned toward the sun—napping. A few joggers race around the edge, while family groups make their way toward the picnic tables in the trees farther to the west. A moppet on a tricycle struggles with the soft surface of the path, then dismounts and begins to pull his vehicle. No one is stretched out on the grass, of course; *pelouse interdite* signs at strategic locations warn the public to keep off the grass.

The Baron Georges-Eugène Haussmann might enjoy the view were he to stand with Jane Jacobs near the edge of the Grand Cours du Louvre, looking toward the Jardin beyond. Behind them are the pale gray stone buildings of the Louvre, with its glass pyramid entrance rising in the middle of the starkly bare square. A long line of people is waiting to descend into the biggest museum in the world. Slightly to the north a group of tourists takes turns shooting pictures of themselves in front of the glass structure designed by I. M. Pei which is either—take your pick—an abomination or an elegant twentieth-century addition to the complex of monumental buildings that has changed continually through more than five centuries.

The Baron would not be at all displeased with what he sees. "The present generation doesn't realize what this part of Paris was like before its complete transformation," the Baron might say to Jane Jacobs. He points with his cane to the north, toward the Nouveau Louvre, beyond which the fine six-story buildings of the rue de Rivoli can been glimpsed. When he began his work in 1852 the area just outside the limits of the garden to the north was a jumble of small buildings and twisting lanes.

"Beyond that stood a disgusting quarter, composed of sordid houses, through which ran narrow alleys," the Baron says. The medieval slum extended from the rue St-Honoré, now the site of some of Paris's most elegant shops, south to the Place du Carrousel, where in the seventeenth century Louis XIV organized a grand equestrian spectacle in honor of the marriage of his son and, some say, in order to impress his mistress. When Haussmann was a young man the grand Place de la Colonnade on the other, eastern side of the Louvre was also filled with a shantytown that extended all the way to the Hôtel de Ville. The lanes were open sewers, and "the rue des Teinturiers (dyers) was so narrow that the worm-eaten façade of one of the houses, composed of pieces of wood covered by rough plaster, was only upright because it was leaning on the house opposite.

"No," he says, looking at Jane Jacobs with satisfaction, "those who didn't, like me, travel around the old Paris of that time can't have a real appreciation of what it was like."

Jane Jacobs always had something to say—all her life she had imaginary conversations with history's great thinkers—but she will not respond quite yet. She has never spent more than a few days in Paris, and more than one once she declined to comment on the city because she felt she didn't know it well enough. But she knows about the problems of nineteenth-century cities; mud and manure were plagues, she admits several times in her writings.

The Baron by all accounts was gallant. His memoir, written shortly before his death in 1891, contains many anecdotes involving him and lively, intelligent women to whom he explains one or another factor of his life and work. It is likely, were he or Jane Jacobs younger, that he would offer to walk her around his city, so he could explain what he had accomplished. But if we are imagining them as people in the fullness of age, a walk, even a short promenade, would be impossible. He, like so many men of his generation, became stout, and she, although wiry as a young woman and a great walker, developed severe problems with her knees as she aged. Her admirers cherish memories of her storming up to the microphone during a meeting question period, clunking along

At the site of the present-day Square Monge, Paris, 1858 . The street—
rue Traversine vers la Montagne Ste-Geneviève—is mentioned as early as 1300.

The Jardin des Tuileries in May 2008. One place where Parisians and visitors have enjoyed themselves for centuries.

with her walker or a cane.

So let us leave them in our imagination sitting in the Jardin, while we stroll across the front of the Louvre and out to the Seine to look toward the Île de la Cité. It is a good place to begin to talk about Paris, because the city exists here because of the river and its islands.

Archeological discoveries and Julius Caesar's Gallic Wars attest to a settlement for more than two thousand years where the Seine makes a lazy loop northward as it cuts its way through the basically flat land that is northern France. For thousands of years before that, the rushing water had taken the easiest course, running around intrusions of harder rock to leave the hills now called Montagne Ste-Geneviève on the Left Bank and Menilmont, Montmartre and Chaillot on the Right Bank. When recorded history begins, several islands dotted the river at the northernmost point of the loop, while marshy lowland extended north as far as the hills. The invading armies of Julius Caesar found a clan of Celts, the Parisii, settled on the islands which were both easy to defend and a good place to cross the Seine. Caesar's *Gallic Wars* tells how the Roman commander Labenius burnt the settlement on what is now the Île de la Cité in 52 BCE. Some recent excavations have uncovered more evidence of this society, including a column (now at the Musée national du moyen âge, the Cluny Museum) dedicated to a god not unlike Jupiter dating from the period. But it wasn't until after the Roman Empire established itself in Gaul that the outlines of the Paris of the future become clearer.

The Romans called the settlement Lutetia. They rejected a site on an island in the Seine because of the risk of flooding, and built on the highland dominated by Montagne Ste-Geneviève. The hill, now crowned by the Panthéon, offers good views of the Seine Valley, even though it only rises about 30 meters (100 feet) above the river. In many respects the site is like other sites the Romans chose for their colonial cities. At Lyon, for example, Lugudium enjoyed tremendous views on heights of the west side of the confluence of the Rhône and the Saône. Both locations are surrounded by relatively flat plateaus which could be cultivated easily, and across which the Roman roads could roll, straight and strong, to other parts of the empire. The Romans avoided making roads that went in and out of river valleys because their thoroughfares were designed for marching troops and baggage trains, because descending switchbacks are harder than marching a greater distance on level ground. The roads were built so well they are still used in some places, as distinctive reminders of Roman civilizations as the Latin inscriptions on the porticos of today's public buildings, or the languages which evolved from Latin in the countries born from the old empire.

Just as they had their standards for road-building, the Romans also had ideas about how a city should be laid out, beginning with two main streets set at right angles and aligned more or less on compass points. They had no compasses (they wouldn't be imported from China for another fifteen hundred years or so) but the alignments based on astronomical observations are quite constant. Here in Lutetia the declination is south-southwest to north-northeast, forming a right angle with the Seine in a line with one of the best islands to use as a stepping stone to cross the river.

The remnants of these streets can be seen in Paris today. If the Baron and Jane Jacobs were to cross the Seine to the Left Bank and stroll in front of the Sorbonne, they'd be following an old Roman road; in 1921 excavations to install gas mains along Rue St-Jacques uncovered Roman paving blocks beneath pavement dating from Haussmann's glory days.

How aware the Baron was of the existence of these Roman vestiges is unclear, but he certainly came to many of the same conclusions about the best way to design a city as had those pioneers of the earlier grand civilization. Both the plan of Lutetia and Haussmann's schemes make the focus of the city a grand crossroads at its center, where wide roads, carrying traffic in and out of the city, meet. Instead of the heights of the Left Bank, however, Haussmann chose to put the crossing on the Right Bank, where the city had grown in the centuries after Rome fell. In the end, he also duplicated the Roman pattern on the Left Bank, because the great north-south boulevard he planned to line up with the north-south thoroughfare on the Right Bank crosses the rue des Écoles only meters away from the Romans' grand crossroads.

The Baron's work, however, lay far in the future when the Romans were building Lutetia. It was a regional center for the better part of three centuries. Its inhabitants enjoyed water piped more than 15 kilometers (9.3 miles) from sources purer than the Seine. The water supplied at least three bath and gymnasium complexes that appear to have been open not only to the upper class of Roman citizens, but also to slaves: one of the perks of living in a Roman city, even in a Roman city so far from Rome, was public services.

But by the end of the fourth century CE the Romans were withdrawing, and urban development retreated to the islands on the Seine.

The city by now had come to be known as Paris, after the Parisii. As raids by German tribes increased on the frontier of the Roman Empire, the city's strategic importance also increased. It welcomed several Roman emperors who were there on campaigns to secure the empire's border, including Julian I, known as Julian the Apostate, who called it "my lovely Lutetia," no matter what the locals called it, and whose troops proclaimed him Caesar there in 361.

The Île de la Cité, where thousands of tourists now visit Notre-Dame Cathedral every day, was fortified with a wall 2.5 meters (8 feet) thick; part of the southern gate was uncovered in 1984 during construction of a subway line. The defenses, bolstered over time, proved relatively good. The Normans were stopped from taking the Cité more than once in the 880s, although unprotected holdings and villages on the Left Bank were sacked. After these attacks the Right Bank became the center of activity. References to walls around particular neighborhoods and even to a wall around the entire town are frequent in texts from the period, but no physical evidence has so far been uncovered.

The Louvre, where we left the Baron and Ms. Jacobs, was originally a fortress built outside the wall erected by King Philipe-Auguste at the end of the twelfth century. If we were to enter the museum today and follow the subterranean passages we could visit what has been excavated of the original fortress. With thick walls and dungeons, it was the safe place where the king stored his treasure, although he lived on the Île de la Cité. The wall he built is still visible elsewhere in the city, particularly on the Left Bank where one remnant is protected by glass at the entrance to a fire station. It looks like just a stack of flat stones with no sign announcing that it was part of an important line of defense against invasions during the days of Richard the Lion-hearted, when England and France fought frequently and the English held parts of Normandy for decades.

Modern Paris is as much a product of its walls as it is of the curve in the Seine and the islands in the river. The city's history in many respects is one of walls fulfilling their function of protecting citizens in times of war. In times of peace, though, the walls became constraints on growth. Kings and governments tried to limit construction beyond the walls, but as threats and troubles passed, residents were tempted to build outside as space inside filled up with orchards and gardens being built over.

When another period of conflict arrived, particularly as the science of war evolved and weapons changed, a new, stronger wall enclosing the larger city seemed imperative. One was built during the Hundred Years War, the long conflict between France and England which ended in 1453 just before Europe was to launch itself into the exploration and conquest of the rest of the world. The old wall around Paris was not much protection against siege machines and longbows. First moats were dug to surround Philip Auguste's wall, and then in the early sixteenth century Charles V built a new wall on the Right Bank about a half a kilometer beyond the earlier wall, enclosing the Louvre and the Bastille.

What lay beyond the wall was the suburbs—the *faubourgs*, the *banlieues*. Many of their churches and the pattern of their streets are still visible in the heart of Paris, even though their names sound ironic today. For example, the densely populated Goutte d'Or neighborhood, today just north of the elevated Métro line and west of the Gare du Nord and its industrial surroundings, gets its name from the excellent wine made once upon a time from the grapes growing on its southward-facing slopes.

By the mid-seventeenth century pressure was mounting again inside the city for more space. Many large estates within the wall that had been owned by religious orders or members of the aristocracy had been subdivided and built on, and building continued in the villages outside the wall. In places, the wall itself was falling to ruin, opening up the land beyond it for easy development. By the 1630s, a new line of fortification was needed, and the Fosses jaunes, the yellow moats, were built. This time more of the Left Bank was enclosed, and the remains of the previous wall were demolished, leaving a band of vacant land some 90 meters (300 feet) wide which eventually became the arc of grand boulevards which curve around the center of Paris today.

The next wall built was not designed to protect the city, but to facilitate the collection of duty on goods entering it. Begun in the 1790s,

The Louvre seen from the Left Bank of the Seine in the 14th century.
From the *Très Riches heures du Duc de Barry*, month of October.

The Barrière blanche in 1855: customs duties were collected on merchandise entering the city of Paris after the *mur d'octroi* was built in 1790.

le *mur d'octroi* featured elaborate gates and a wooden palisade more than two meters high. Beyond it a band of land about 100 meters (330 feet) wide was not supposed to be built upon, but was frequently crossed by smugglers. The grandiose gates caused many ordinary folk to grumble; the gate near the Bastille was the object of protests in the days preceding the taking of the Bastille in July 1789, which marked the beginning of the French Revolution.

By the restoration of the monarchy in 1830, the fears for the safety of an unprotected city had surfaced again, leading to the construction of the Enceinte de Thiers beyond the *mur d'octroi*. When Haussmann arrived on the scene, it was clear that the city should include all the area between the new wall and the old customs wall, which was torn down, to much popular satisfaction.

This pattern of repeated wall construction, growing population, and then movement beyond the previous barriers produced a jumble of streets. In many places streets dead-ended where earlier walls had been. Other streets fed into larger ones that had led to places where a gate once opened to the countryside. In parts of the enlarged city, streets also reflected the layout of old villages that had been incorporated into Paris, while in the dense center of the city, streets twisted and turned past buildings packed as closely together as possible. The Romans would hardly recognize what Lutetia had become more than 1400 years later.

In one respect, though, the city was not at all different: the speed of travel. Horses had been fastest things on the Roman roads, and that still held true for the streets of Paris when Napoléon III summoned Haussmann to Paris to take the post of *préfet*. Railroads had begun to revolutionize intercity transport, and their stations and sorting yards were taking up more and more space in Paris. Conveyances powered by anything other than horses for travel within cities were still decades away, however. Indeed, horses probably traveled faster in Lutetia than they did in Paris when Haussmann arrived, because the narrow streets were so choked with wagons and carriages that traffic usually moved no faster than a man could walk. The lack of speed did not matter for the vast majority of men, not to mention women and children, since they always walked. And because a short walk to work was better than a long one, people lived as close as they could to their employment.

Take the following morning scene just inside the gate on the Goutte

41

d'Or, described by Emile Zola in *The Dram Shop* (*L'Assommoir*), his novel of working-class life in the 1850s:

> At the barrier the tramp of the herds going to work resonated in the cold of the morning. One recognized the locksmiths by their blue canvas work shirts, the masons with their white coveralls, the painters in their smocks with long shirts hanging out below. From a distance the crowd looked dusty and faded to a neutral tone where washed-out blue or dirty gray were the predominant colors. Now a worker stopped to relight his pipe, while around him the others continued to march onwards, without a laugh or a word spoken to a comrade. Their grubby faces all looked toward Paris which, one by one, devoured them.

Then a little later when the shops were open,

> ... the flood of work shirts coming down from the hill stopped, and only a few laggards rushed past the barrier. ... The working girls—the metal polishers, the seamstresses, the florists—took the place of the workmen. They hugged themselves in their thin dresses, trotting down the exterior boulevards; they walked in groups of three or four, chatting with animation, laughing lightly, darting bright glances from side to side. They were followed by one, all alone, looking pale and serious, walking along the edge of the wall carefully to avoid the filthy streams of water in the road. Then the shop workers passed, blowing on their fingers, gnawing at their penny's worth of bread as they walked. Along came the lanky young folk, their jackets too short and with rings around their eyes still fuzzy with sleep; the little old men shuffled past, their pale faces worn from long hours in the office, checking their watches to time their walks down to the last second.

The streets they walked on were often unpaved and usually had no sidewalks. In rainy weather "A few moments were enough for the roadway to be covered in puddles, a thick mud, trodden by passersby, made the sidewalks sticky," Zola writes elsewhere. "A gust of wet air, the breath of the old quarter, came from the street; it seemed that the stream of umbrellas flowed all the way to the shop's counters, that the pavement with its mud and dirty puddles came into the building, overcome by the mustiness of the old pavement."

These streets were not walked by the gentry. Another Zola character says when her father comments on her lovely white dress that "a lady could be quite inconvenienced, wearing that on the sidewalks," "but, Father, one never goes out on foot."

Having fine horses and a carriage were the equivalent of driving BMWs and Hummers today: a sign of wealth as well as a convenience. Haussmann himself had a two-horse coupé and a victoria for his personal use as well as a berline and a calèche for his family as perks of the office of préfet. (The rented carriages came with two coachmen and four horses, and cost 14,000 FR a year, which equaled about 7,000 Euros or $12,000 CDN.)

Carriages waiting outside the Bourse, Paris 1860. The volume of horse-drawn vehicles in central Paris caused huge traffic jams in the middle of the nineteenth century.

This was the period in which Paris became the hub of rail traffic in France, with tracks entering it from all compass points. To send merchandise from Lyon to Bordeaux, for example, required shipping to Paris and then transferring the load to another railroad line at a station across the city. The narrow streets made such transfers a noisy nightmare. They were bad enough for the carters and the companies trying to transport goods, but equally important for what was to follow was the fact that the continual traffic crossed sections of the Right Bank where the well-off lived. In part to escape congestion, the wealthy had begun moving out of the center to the west and north, which did not please those with an economic interest in center-city property. In addition, France's tumultuous politics of the post-Bonaparte period led to popular uprisings in 1830 and 1848. When the forces of order tried to move troops around the city to put down insurgents they found their progress continually blocked by twisting streets where barricades were easily constructed.

The Haussmannian approach to correcting these problems was a plan for redevelopment that was breathtaking in its scope. During a period of less than twenty years the Paris of winding streets, of multistory apartment blocks backing on filthy courtyards, of cultural jewels hidden from view by slums, was substantially swept away. Other city makeovers, like Christopher Wren's plans for rebuilding London after the Great Fire of 1666, were either smaller, not completed, or spread out over so long a period as to approach the slow pace of organic change. Haussmann's rapid accomplishments would become the reference point for politicians and urban planners in the future, for good or ill.

Robert Moses, Jane Jacobs' nemesis in New York, compared himself to Haussmann more than once. But although the adjective "Haussmannian" is commonly used to refer to the great reorganizing of Paris, Haussmann is not the only one to whom credit or blame should be assigned. Napoléon III guided him, and it is safe to say that without the emperor's enthusiastic support Haussmann's changes would have been limited to the continuation of projects already begun plus a little tinkering with traffic patterns.

Napoléon III had plans to change Paris long before he was elected president of France's First Republic in December 1848. Educated in Germany and Switzerland, he had spent most of his life in exile, and in

Construction of the rue de l'Opéra in 1876. Haussmann's projects required hundreds of workers and tens of thousands of francs.

the early 1840s published a theoretical work, *L'Extinction de pauperisme*. Before becoming involved in uprisings in France, he also championed republican causes in Italy and twice took refuge in English-speaking countries, first in the United States and then in Great Britain.

The year 1848 was a revolutionary one, with uprisings not only in France, but in what would become Italy and Germany. The establishment of the French First Republic was intended to counter dissatisfaction of the working classes and to provide stability desired by the middle and upper classes. Napoléon III was the choice of royalists of all stripes when presidential elections were held. He arrived in office bursting with ideas for bettering the lot of the French, many of them gleaned from his experience elsewhere.

London, where he lived from 1846 to just before his return, affected him particularly. Street-lighting, sewer systems, water supply, better transportation and new wide roads for the center of Paris were all on his agenda. The first step would be completion of two streets started decades before—rue Rambuteau and the western part of rue de Rivoli near the Louvre. Linking the new rail stations was also high on his list. In addition, the major centers of learning and instruction on the Left

Bank could only be reached by tortuous routes, twisting up and down streets from earlier periods of the city's history.

He began by commissioning a model building, the Cité Napoléon, in 1849. He also set up competitions to encourage social housing projects. But it was clear that more must be done, and the emperor (as he became in December, 1852 after a coup d'état in which he seized power from the National Assembly) went looking for a good administrator to take the post of *préfet* of Paris. Haussmann had shown his administrative talents in Bordeaux and elsewhere. He had also made a very favorable impression on the man he frequently called "my mentor" during the referendum campaign in which Napoléon III asked the nation to endorse a return to an imperial state; enthusiastic crowds had turned out in great numbers to greet the leader wherever Haussmann was in charge.

In 1853 when Haussmann arrived in Paris to take the job, he had spent fifteen years in regional administration, but his roots were in the capital. Born to a Protestant family originally from Alsace, he spent his early childhood at his grandparents' country place, but as an adolescent he had to make the trek across Paris from the comfortable Chaussé d'antin neighborhood to school on the Left Bank. It was a long and circuitous walk. He had to leave home at 7 a.m., he did not have time to go home in the middle of the day, and his route took him through some of the worst parts of the city. The Île de la Cité, where the courts and the cathedral of Notre Dame were hidden by a motley collection of haphazardly constructed buildings, made a strong impression on him.

Nothing remains of that today. The courtyard in front of Notre Dame is a great open space, deep enough for photographers to back up and get pictures of the whole of the cathedral. The other buildings are solid, beautifully redolent of a past which must have been glorious.

Were the conversation to turn in that direction, the Baron might tell Jane Jacobs how pleased he was to do away with the slums that existed when he began his work. The "sordid group of huts" on the Île de la Cité were "the homes of thieves and murderers who assembled there to mock the Police correctionielle and the Cour d'Assises," he might say, adding with satisfaction, "I had the joy of razing them from top to bottom."

Jane Jacobs would find the destruction of hundreds of people's dwellings, no matter how dilapidated, appalling. Her sharp, intelligent face—Robert Fulford, who knew her in Toronto, compared her to an eagle—might turn toward him, accusingly. "Razed?" she might ask. "Did it help anything?" A hundred years after Haussmann tore down that slum, she could tell him, North Americans had "a wistful myth that if only we had enough money to spend—the figure is usually put at a hundred billion dollars—we could wipe out all our slums in ten years … and perhaps even solve the traffic problem." But, she would tell the Baron, it was not true, it turned out to be all wishful thinking. The reality was that twentieth-century urban development amounted to a waste of money and the destruction of much of what was good in cities.

Critics made that kind of comment even in Haussmann's day, but he paid little attention as he went about destroying much of what had been medieval Paris. As Léonce Reynaud, professor at the École Polytechnique, wrote as early as 1863, "(the city) guards invaluable evidence of the phases through which it has passed. … These souvenirs of the past are not read only in the monuments; they're found, or rather they are felt, on all sides: in the general layout of the city, in the squares, in the promenades …The plan, so complicated that one can find no law in it and which at first glance appears to have been drawn by chance, in fact has innumerable causes each with its own value, and which have been worked on by time."

Haussmann and Napoléon III, however, were convinced that what they were doing would dramatically improve the lives of their contemporaries and of Parisians of the future. Part of their passion for change came from true, if perhaps misguided, altruism, but other motives were present. Napoléon III believed that popular unrest was best fought by making things better for ordinary folk, *le petit peuple*. But he also listened with an attentive ear to those in the wealthier classes who had a vested interest in keeping the center of Paris prosperous and unencumbered by the waves of poor workers and their families who were attracted to the city, its railroads and jobs. As the better-off moved out, the gentry and upper bourgeoisie feared that only the poorer classes would remain in the center, which would then become another huge slum.

That was exactly what was being asserted about American cities when Jane Jacobs became active in urban affairs. Indeed White Flight from cities in the U.S. and the urban renewal which razed large areas of them have much in common with what happened in mid-nineteenth-century Paris. But, unlike the situation in the United States a century later, the people flooding into Paris seeking work were no different in skin color from those who lived there already. They came first from northern France and Flanders, which had been the scene of decades of battles prior to and during the Napoleonic wars. As the railroad system developed, they arrived from further afield: the novels of Émile Zola are full of characters from small towns who find themselves getting off the train at one of the great railroad stations (which Napoléon III called the "real gates" of Paris), not knowing what to do next. Many of them would find a room in one of the five- and six-story buildings which were the rule already in the center of Paris. There would be no running water available above the first floor, and no windows in many of the rooms.

But, for some, the insalubrious lodging promised better times. In *The Dram Shop* Zola paints just such a place, a large five-story building not far from the boulevard Goutte d'Or. The neighborhood had already changed considerably from the time when the hillside was covered with vineyards. The building was "a big bare cube the color of mud, with its sides not stuccoed and with the same interminable bareness as the walls of a prison. Around it rows of waiting building stones look like abandoned jaws, yawning in the void."

Gervaise, the novel's main character, doesn't notice this nor does she see the pale pink stream running under the courtyard door from the dyer's workshop inside.

"The building didn't look ugly to her," Zola writes. Viewed from the interior courtyard "there were corners of gaiety: a cage of canaries from which fell a pleasant chirping sound. Shaving mirrors caught the sun like round stars. Down below a carpenter was singing, accompanied by the regular whistling of his plane. Children were laughing and women were sitting peacefully sewing … The only thing was that the courtyard was a little damp. If Gervaise lived here, she would want one of the apartments at the back, on the sunny side." It smelled of poverty, but since the sharp smell from the dyers dominated, she thought it smelled better than the place she was living then. "And she had already chosen her window, the window on the left, where there was a little wooden box, planted with climbing beans, whose thin shoots had begun to roll themselves around a framework of strings."

But when she moves into the building, it is hardly the paradise she hopes for. Unfortunately that was the case for many people. Napoléon III considered it to be his mission to do away with this kind of housing, to encourage the working classes to move outside the center, and to cut through the dense city landscape in order to let in "light and air."

The new, wide streets themselves were to be built in three great waves. When Haussmann arrived in Paris, Napoléon III already had a map of much of what was to be done. Color-coded in blue, red, yellow and green, it was the fruit of considerable reflection and of a competence that many observers thought lacking in Napoléon III's other policies. However that may be, this map—revised as the years passed, to be sure—guided road-building in Paris until the beginning of the twentieth century. Haussmann wrote that he never approved any project before it received Napoléon III's blessing and was duly entered on his map.

The construction of a major north-south route on the Right Bank was one of the first projects on the list. Initially Napoléon III thought it possible to merely widen rue St-Denis to make it broader and to bring the buildings into better alignment so that the modernized street would not have zigs and zags. But after a little discussion, Haussmann and his team realized that it would probably be easier to cut new streets than to play with existing ones, given the cost and trouble of expropriating property. Rue de Sébastopol, opened in 1859, leads from the Seine to the Gare de l'Est, and is only a little to the west of rue St-Denis. From the air the difference is striking, though. Rue de Sébastopol and its extension boulevard Strasbourg run broad and straight, while the older street is much narrower and meanders slightly, reflecting the haphazard way the street was developed over the years.

In all, nearly ninety new roadways were constructed under the plans developed by Haussmann, although a few, like the boulevard which bears his name, weren't completed until just before World War I. In the center of Paris nearly twenty thousand buildings were torn down between 1852 and 1869, while forty-three thousand new ones were constructed in the same period. How this translated into dwelling units is not clear since the buildings were usually divided up into apartments which might contain several rooms—or just one. Much of the new construction was in the suburbs. Whole neighborhoods just beyond the *mur d'octroi* filled in as the displaced sought new places to live.

This movement of the working classes outward was viewed with approval by most contemporary observers. The Baron could quote one who wrote, "Will it be necessary to let the workers squat without air, without sunlight in the hideous lanes whose unhealthiness is the odious and permanent companion of epidemics?" The municipal administration "always humanely inspired, has encouraged this quite understandable emigration by giving these (new) neighborhoods what they have lacked until now. Streets are being paved, sidewalks constructed, fire hydrants installed where needed and, soon, thanks to projects which are currently being studied and which will certainly be undertaken, this part of the city will have nothing for which to envy other outlying neighborhoods."

Some of these newly settled *quartiers* were close to factories, railroad yards and other establishments which employed many workers. Other areas became magnets for industry because of the available work force. But public transportation, even when it was available, was often too expensive for the working folk to take, so many, if not most, walked to work.

This being Sunday, most of the walkers today in the Jardin des Tuileries are not on their way to or from work. They come from all classes, drawn by the gardens' fame, or the museum, or a temporary exhibit of large modern sculptures which takes pride of place this particular weekend. The Baron and Jane Jacobs, were they to sit in chairs drawn close together, would have a prospect as pleasant as it was in the middle of the nineteenth century. Several of Zola's working-class characters passed their Sunday *congés* here, because it was one of the few green spaces within walking distance of the crowded streets where they lived.

The Baron was disappointed that more ordinary folk didn't use the two large green spaces, the Bois de Boulogne and the Bois de Vincennes, which he and Napoléon III established. The reason, he admitted, was "the distance, the time needed to go and come and the cost of even the most economical of transports which ended up being too much to be done very often. But it is a pleasure to see that on each holiday the popular masses invade the two woods, spread out all over the parks and enjoy themselves, feeling that they are at home there."

Jane Jacobs might say something about the complicated relationship between parks and their neighborhoods at this point. She could add that an unused park bordered by boring streets is a recipe for an unsafe urban space. The Baron, however, would prefer to laud Napoléon III and his vision for Paris:

It is a real happiness for those who faithfully remember the August author of these immense works, whose usefulness surpasses even their grandeur. One can be legitimately proud having known that he understood and heartily endorsed these enterprises to the point of obtaining his complete approval.

This is, Jane Jacobs might say, an excellent example of the Guardian attitude, of which she wrote extensively after she'd written her three books about cities. Her judgement would only be reinforced if the Baron went on:

During his very long stay in England, the Emperor was struck by the contrast between the well-kept squares in London, and the sordid state of the slums where the families of workers lived crowded together. He saw there a sort of mute protest by the young against bad habits of which they saw far too many examples among their parents.

Contact with green spaces would through a process of slow seduction "lead these offspring of the city's working poor to better habits and (lead to) the gradual amelioration of the morals of the working classes by the example of nicely kept green spaces."

That is why, the Baron said, "he instructed me not to waste any opportunity to make squares and green spaces throughout Paris in order to give places for relaxation and recreation of families, for all children, rich and poor, as he had seen in London.

"Hopes, illusions, if you will, generous illusions—which I didn't entirely share" led the Emperor to think that these creations "could not help but exercise positive influence on the masses." The Baron notes, though, that he saw little evidence of this.

Jane Jacobs might agree: "There is no direct, simple relationship between good housing and good behavior, a fact which the whole tale of the Western world's history, the whole collection of our literature, and the whole fund of observation open to any of us should long since have made evident," she said. She didn't think that health benefits are inherent in green spaces and the opening of the streets. The idea that parks and squares are the lungs of the city is "science fiction nonsense," because "it takes about three acres of woods to absorb as much carbon dioxide as four people exhale in breathing, cooking and heating. The oceans of air circulating about us, not parks, keep cities from suffocating." Come now, she might say to the Baron as she said to many other people, look around and you'll see.

What I see, the Baron might respond, is a magnificent city. He could wave a sheaf of appreciations made over more than century of what was wrought in the City of Light during his tenure, or according to his plans after he was forced out of office for overspending his budget. "I was criticized for talking about being able to see the Column of the Bastille and the Dome of the Panthéon," he says. "The Emperor, who so frequently showed such good taste in many things, told me I was too artistic in this matter, too inclined to sacrifice the corrections of the street line and too desirous of finding good points of view than could be reasonably justified for the public road. 'In London,' he told me, 'they only seek to satisfy the need of traffic circulation as well as possible.' My invariable response was: 'Sir, the Parisians are not the English; they deserve better.'"

He gestures across the Jardins towards the end of the Île de la Cité and tells Jane Jacobs that one of the things he is most proud of is the new bridge across the Seine which meets the bottom of the boulevard St-Michel, and the beautiful fountain in the square. That is "my revenge on the melancholic spectacle which I had to face for four long years as I did my studies," he says.

Jane Jacobs, who never got a postsecondary degree, is unlikely to protest that the fountain is nothing more than a lovely landmark. She recognizes beauty. She worked for years as a staff writer and editor for *Architectural Review*, and an appreciation of fine elements in the cityscape is something you acquire there, if you do not have it before. But what would likely impress her more is the lively street life where the boulevard St-Michel meets the quays on the Seine. People on streets are what interest her, and were she to spend more than a few days in Paris, she might ask how this city became probably the most compact and pleasant city to walk in, in the world, despite—or because—of what Haussmann and Napoléon III did. What is the relation between the way Paris pleases the walker and the resident today, and Haussmann's plans for it? What does this success have to do with what Jane Jacobs would have liked to see for cities and city-dwellers everywhere? What are the lessons that might be used to make our cities strong and walkable in the coming century?

CHAPTER 4

Jane Jacobs in New York and Toronto

THE SOUPY HEAT of New York in June weighs down the evening. It's a night to drink beer on stoops, which is just what two young men are doing, passing a bottle back and forth. They're talking quietly, making plans for where to go and what to do later on this Saturday night. Down on the sidewalk a thin woman in Bermuda shorts and a sleeveless blouse holds a girl about three on her hip while she talks to two other women wearing summer dresses. The child's hair lies in tiny, damp curls on her forehead and she leans away from her mother, as if being in contact with another warm body is too much.

A few cars pass on the street, but don't stop. There is no space free to park. The sidewalks, however, are busy with people going somewhere in the light from the street lamps. Windows are open—this is the end of the 1960s and air conditioning is rare—so the sound of *The Lawrence Welk Show*'s last waltz floats down, fighting with the Rolling Stones' "I Can't Get No Satisfaction" blasting from another apartment.

Jane Jacobs lives around the corner with her husband and three kids. Washington Square Park is a few blocks away. It appears that—possibly, just maybe, we'll have to wait and see to make sure—residents of Greenwich Village and the West Village have finally beaten back a freeway that would slice through the neighborhood.

This is a long way geographically from Paris and a hundred years after Baron Haussmann remade that city. There are similarities, though, that Jane Jacobs may never have commented on, but which will fuel the debate about cities, particularly the walkable city, for decades to come.

On the equivalents in New York City's planning offices of Napoléon III's color-coded map, this neighborhood is currently tagged as a slum. There will be a number of redevelopment projects in coming years, and New York University will claim more land for itself. But the future is looking brighter thanks to a book Jane Jacobs wrote a few years before about what is wrong with American cities in the mid-twentieth century, and because of citizens' protests that she helped organize.

Jane Jacobs told interviewers that she was enchanted by Paris, that it seemed familiar to her when she first visited because she had seen so many paintings and photographs of it. But she avoided making comments on how it was organized or whether it could teach North Americans anything. Indeed, she neatly finessed a leading question from urban affairs writer James Howard Kunstler when he asked her why North Americans hadn't laughed at the idea of tearing down the centers of their cities in the 1950s and '60s the way Parisians laughed at proposals to raze the Right Bank and rebuild a "modern" city.

"Lots of people did laugh," she retorted, and she, of course, was one of the loudest. Her book *The Death and Life of Great American Cities* laid down the gauntlet in the first sentence: "This book is an attack on current city planning and rebuilding." It became the definitive book on what was wrong with the kind of development that took the world by storm in the mid-twentieth century. Inspired by Swiss architect Le Corbusier, who advocated apartment towers set in green lawns as the way to make cities healthier and to integrate motor vehicles into them, "radiant city" plans were adopted everywhere governments wanted to clear substandard housing and rehouse the poor. Among the motivations was the desire to eliminate pockets of poverty, a very Haussmannian goal, which in the northern cities of the U.S. most often meant moving African-Americans out. Practically without exception the projects failed, and Jane Jacobs was the first to figure out why. Her book quickly became a classic in urban affairs commentary, using New York as its laboratory and example.

At that point she'd lived in the Big Apple for nearly thirty years, ever since she moved at age eighteen from the small city in Pennsylvania where she was born, to seek adventure and a writing career. New York was the logical choice for a young woman with ambition and a lot of energy, even though in the Depression year of 1934, when she arrived, times were bad.

New York was the largest city in the Western Hemisphere, the United States' center of commerce and culture, the home of the Great White Way, the place where the action was. Yet it was relatively new compared to European cities. The year that Europeans stumbled on Manhattan, 1609, there had been a settlement at Paris for more than seventeen hundred years, and what Henry Hudson saw when he sailed up the river which now bears his name looked nearly uninhabited. The island, called Mannahatta ("land of many hills") by the four hundred or so Lenni Lenape people living there, was covered with hemlock forests interspersed with a few clearings that abounded with "Grasse and Flowers, and goodly Trees ... and very sweet smells came from them," according to Hudson's first mate Robert Juet. Europeans who visited in the years to follow noted the fine grass and called it "a land excellent and agreeable, full of noble forest trees and grape vines."

Very little of the landscape of that time remains, but one vestige is as clearly evident now as the tracks of Roman roads are in France: the trail the Lenni Lenape took to get from one end of the island to the other. It's called Broadway today, and cuts diagonally across the neat grid of New York's streets, avoiding the high points and the swampy middle, most of which were filled in or leveled long ago. The grid is the result of some far-reaching surveying done at the beginning the nineteenth century. It is emblematic of the difference between old cities in Europe and elsewhere, and newer ones that have sprung up since the Age of Exploration began.

That difference is that the new cities were planned from the beginning, while the older ones just grew for most of their existence. Previously only an imperial power like the Romans could insist on rational layout at the beginning of a city's history. Even that order was frequently blurred as time went by, political powers changed, and people built their houses and established their workshops and stores in the interstices of the grand plan. To make order out of urban chaos at a later date required the same sort of political force that Napoléon III and Haussmann exercised.

European migration to the Western Hemisphere coincided with an increasing interest in rational ways to organize life. The principles of the Age of Enlightenment were important for such nation-builders as William Penn and Thomas Jefferson. Within a short time it became common to lay out new settlements on a rational plan, most often on a grid. In a few places, including the English settlements of Savannah and Philadelphia and the Spanish ones of Albuquerque and Buenos

Aires, the layout included squares and space set aside for churches and public buildings. More often, though, the plans were relatively plain rectangular grids formed by streets crossing streets. Often the roadways were laid out with one starting parallel to a lake or waterfront and subsequent streets arranged either parallel or perpendicular to it. Topography often underlay the descriptions of parcels of land; a lot might be said to have as its eastern edge a line extending from a large chestnut tree northward to the outcrop of dark gray rock. By the end of the eighteenth century, however, a still more rational approach based on survey lines and compass headings was adopted in most places to avoid confusion when big trees were cut down and geological features became obscured by erosion or construction. In both the United States and what would become Canada, the survey lines constructed this way could in principle stretch to fill the continent, and eventually did.

In 1803 New York's city commissioners decided to put aside lot descriptions based on topography and grids that were oriented more or less haphazardly. Manhattan had a population of about sixty-five thousand and a heritage of more than a 150 years of piecemeal subdivision and street-plotting. The island is not a clear geometric shape—"New York is much better shaped for a cucumber than a city," one nineteenth-century observer commented—so over the years as larger parcels were cut up and streets laid out with the shoreline as the reference point, several grids developed which had little relation to compass directions. Streets were extended back from the waterfront as the settlements grew until the variously oriented grids began to bump into each other. Some way had to be found to integrate those grids and to govern development on the rest of the island as settlement moved northward.

The City Corporation—more like a private corporation than a city government as North Americans usually understand it now—owned a substantial part of the island, at least 1,300 acres (about 535 hectares). Beginning late in the eighteenth century, parcels were sold off, both to raise money for development of services and to allow private parties to build. In 1789, for example, 200 acres (about 81 hectares) including today's high-rent area bounded by Broadway, Lexington Avenue, 32nd Street and 42nd Street were sold for about $70 an acre to nine purchasers.

The plotting of the complete island took nearly four years. Hackles

The survey ordered by New York City commissioners resulted in a grid of streets being laid over Manhattan in 1807.

were raised wherever the surveyors went. One wrote that on several occasions he had been arrested by the sheriff for trespass and damage done by his crew, and another group of surveyors were once driven off by a woman selling vegetables who bombarded them with artichokes and cabbages.

The survey commission considered departing from the grid pattern by adopting "some of those supposed improvements by circles, ovals, and stars, which certainly embellish a plan, whatever may be their effect as to convenience and utility." But practicality won the day: "A city is to be composed principally of the habitations of men, and ... straight-sided and right-angled houses are the most cheap to build and the most convenient to live in," the surveyors' report says. They may have been influenced by the enormous survey of the entire United States which President Thomas Jefferson had recently mandated. Over the next few years the nation would be measured one 66-foot chain at a time in order to map it and lay out a pattern for settlement based on latitude and longitude.

Along with the grid that extended as far as what is now the Bronx, New York City commissioners laid out a market on the East River side of Manhattan and a large parade ground, but included little other open space. The city was far from green; Washington Square was a cemetery, and the commissioners' own map showed only two or three small squares. What trees the island boasted were only half grown because fifteen years before during the Revolutionary War the British, who were isolated from the mainland, cut down all the trees. George Washington noted in 1781 that "the island is totally stripped."

The Commissioners conceded that not providing for parks and other common space might surprise some:

> Certainly if the city of New York was destined to stand on the side of a small stream such as the Seine or the Thames, a great number of ample places might be needful. But those large arms of the sea which embrace Manhattan island render its situation, in regard to health and pleasure as well as to the convenience of commerce, peculiarly felicitous.

Fifty years later, city fathers would decide that that was a wrong decision, and authorize the establishment of Central Park. (In 1811, the surveyors had expected a population of four hundred thousand by mid-century, but the 1860 census shows more than twice that.) Frederick Law Olmsted and Calvert Vaux were given the job of planning the new park, and Olmsted took a run at changing the development pattern for the northern parts of the island. Noting quite rightly that the grid ran roughshod over topographic features, he argued for preserving some of the area in a more natural state for the emerging middle class which was "struggling to maintain an honorable independence."

The grid prevailed, however, and, a century after Olmsted, Jane Jacobs was very pleased about that. By then Washington Square and its surrounding neighborhood had gone through many transformations. The square itself became an official green space about fifteen years after the Commissioners' plan was adopted, and in the late 1820s and 1830s a row of elegant residences was built on the northern side. It was, wrote Henry James in 1880 in his short novel *Washington Square*, the "ideal of quiet and of genteel retirement," with houses which embodied "the latest results of architectural science." The square contained "a considerable quantity of inexpensive vegetation, enclosed by a wooden paling which increased its rural and accessible appearance." The whole neighborhood, he wrote, had "a kind of established repose which is not of frequent occurrence in other quarters of this long shrill city … It had the look of having had something of a social history."

But the attractions of the Square did not keep New York's better-off classes from moving farther north. As one of James's characters explains, he and his young wife will be buying their first house in another neighborhood. "It's only for three or four years. At the end of three or four years we'll move … I guess we'll move up little by little: when we get tired of one street we'll go higher. So you see we'll always have a new house … They invent everything all over again about every five years, and it's a great thing to keep up with the new things."

By the end of the nineteenth century the south side of the Square had become far less aristocratic. One source says it was "populated with immigrants living in tenement houses." Nevertheless when the centennial of George Washington's inauguration as president of the United States rolled around in 1889, the square was considered the logical place for celebrations in his memory. A wooden arch inspired by the Arc de Triomphe in Paris whipped up such enthusiasm that a permanent 77-foot (23.4-meter) marble version was put up in 1895. Over the next fifty years the Memorial Arch and the Square became much-photographed emblems of New York, even though the surrounding neighborhood continued to go downhill and traffic roared beneath the arch itself. To counter what city officials considered urban blight, funds from post-World War II slum renewal programs were used to raze many buildings to the south of the square for new high-rise housing and for the campus of New York University. Then in the 1960s Robert Moses—the driving force behind both New York's urban renewal programs and its mammoth highway building—decided that his proposed Lower Manhattan Expressway should cut through the neighborhood.

This is when Jane Jacobs shifted from writing freelance articles on architecture to community activism and full-fledged urban criticism, all the while raising three children.

In the exhibition *Block by Block: Jane Jacobs and the Future of New York*, which ran in the fall of 2007, there is a picture of her demonstrating to save Penn Station in New York. She's wearing white gloves and a neat little knee-length sheath dress with a string of beads around her neck. It's 1963, and the woman carrying a placard beside her is similarly well-dressed. Their feet don't show in the photo but it's likely they're wearing high heels because that is what women did in the early 1960s on important occasions, although Jane Jacobs was well on her way at that point to casting aside the trappings of a well-bred young woman. (Jane Kramer would eventually write in *The Village Voice* that Jane "looks rather like a prophet. People who have seen her in action at the Board of Estimate or down on Broome Street rarely forget that clomping, sandaled stride and that straight gray hair flying every which way around a sharp, quizzical face.")

The photograph and the description point up just how much she was a woman of contradictions. She wrote that she had no desire to continue school when she finished high school in her hometown of Scranton, Pennsylvania, although her doctor father and trained-nurse mother insisted that their children each have a career dream—hers was writing or reporting—as well as a backup skill. So she went to secretarial school for six months after high school, and "if I do say so myself I became a good stenographer."

What she learned stood her in good stead when she went to New York, because she couldn't find anything in journalism at first. Every morning she left the house where her sister had already established herself with friends, and looked for work. When nothing panned out, she told an interviewer later, she would spend the rest of the day looking around, sometimes taking the subway and picking a stop arbitrarily to get out and explore. "And one day I found myself in a neighborhood I just liked so much. I was enchanted with this neighborhood, and walked around it all afternoon." When she got back home she told her sister that she'd found the place "where we have to live. And she said, 'Where is it?' And I said, 'I don't know, but you get in the subway and you get out at a place called Christopher Street.'"

Christopher Street is in Greenwich Village. That neighborhood was to become her home for nearly three decades, and it was in the Village that she would develop her ideas about urban places. She and her sister moved there, and she stayed. (After World War II she, her architect husband Robert Hyde Jacobs and their children lived at 555 Hudson Street, a few blocks from the Christopher Street subway station.) She went back to school, taking courses that interested her. She let·her curiosity about cities lead her when she began doing freelance writing for publications like *Vogue* magazine, writing articles on New York's flower, fur, and diamond districts. Between 1942 and 1953 she worked as a feature writer for the Office of Wartime Information and then for *Amerika,* published by the State Department and the Overseas Information Agency.

One book of occasional pieces, interviews, and family letters (*Ideas that Matter: The Worlds of Jane Jacobs,* published by The Ginger Press) includes photos from this period in her life, among them one of a pregnant Jane modeling maternity clothes for the Russian edition of *Amerika.* Many of the other pictures and letters in the book show a Jane who was a sharp observer of the world while building a comfortable, middle-class life. The book has photos of Jane and Bob—who says he met her at a party when she was wearing a "beautiful green woollen dress"—kissing on the sofa, with a group of friends on the roof of Jane's apartment building, on their wedding day two months after they met, and standing with their arms around each other's waist in the yard of Jane's parents' house in Scranton. There also are snapshots of Jane and

After World War II Jane Jacobs and her husband Robert Hyde Jacobs remodeled 555 Hudson in Greenwich Village into a comfortable home for themselves and their three children. The building, however, has been changed back into commercial space.

her children: Jane cuddling a cherubic Jimmy, holding a grinning Ned, and making Christmas cookies, as well as Bob in work clothes in front of 555 Hudson.

But despite this ordinary life, full of what appears to be quite usual post-war prosperity and optimism, Jane was analyzing cities, perhaps without really understanding the importance of what she was doing.

In 1952 the offices of the government publications she was working for were transferred to Washington, so she went looking for a job in

New York. "My husband subscribed to *Architectural Forum,* and I had become a regular reader of it, first out of curiosity, and then because I liked it very much," she explains in a little autobiographical essay. The other possibility was *Natural History,* but since *Architectural Forum* paid more, she applied, did a trial assignment and found herself hired as associate editor and resident expert on schools and hospitals. "I was utterly baffled at first, being supposed to make sense of great, indigestible rolls of working drawings and plans," she wrote. Her husband helped her decipher them, and after a while she began writing on city planning and rebuilding, where the fresh eye she brought to what was going on led her to conclusions that were startling. "It soon became obvious to me, as I looked at what was being built and what was working, that city planning had nothing to do with how cities worked successfully in real life."

She might have continued criticizing on a case-by-case basis except that in 1956 (the year after the Jacobs' third child, Mary Hyde, was born), her boss had to find a substitute for a presentation he was to give at Harvard. She was enlisted over her protests— "I had awful stage fright"—to fill in, but insisted that she be allowed to speak on what she wanted to. "It was a real ordeal for me," she told an interviewer years later. "I have no memory of giving it. I just went into some kind of hypnosis and said this thing I had memorized. And sat down and it was a big hit because nobody had heard anybody saying these things before, apparently."

The talk led to an article in *Fortune,* which led to a grant from the Rockefeller Foundation, and then another when the first ran out. Two years and four months later, in the fall of 1961 *The Death and Life of Great American Cities* was published. The book has no illustrations, because, she began. "The scenes that illustrate this book are all about us. For illustrations, please look closely at real cities." Then she went on to speak plainly about truths that nobody had dared to face. "The economic rationale of current city rebuilding is a hoax," she wrote.

And "all the art and science of city planning are helpless to stem decay" which was rampant in American cities. The street, rather than the super block of high-rise public housing and the plaza-surrounded, glass and granite office tower, is the basis on which a healthy city depends, she contended.

The first part of the book was drawn from observation of her own neighborhood, its sidewalks (wide enough for people to loiter on), its parks (sometimes inviting when there are enough different sorts of people using them throughout the day), and its healthy excitement. Because there was a mix of housing, retail, and commercial uses, people had reason to be on the streets at all hours. Neighbors were remembered, strangers were noticed, children were protected. Parks can be nice, but they're not as important as a streetscape where people feel free to tarry and talk, to shop and kibitz.

Long before *Six Degrees of Separation* or Malcolm Gladwell's theories about the importance of key people in the passing of information and influence, Jane and her sister were speculating on how many people it would take to get a message from a native of the Solomon Islands in the South Pacific to a cobbler in Rock Island, Illinois. They found it pretty easy to guess how a message might be relayed at either end of the chain, but they discovered that they needed "hop-skip" people in the middle who would make the jump from one world to another. Eleanor Roosevelt was the best link, because she knew "the most unlikely people." Neighborhoods are like that, Jacobs decided later, needing people who serve as bridges for contact between different corners, different groups.

To an outsider who is not clued into the life brimming over in a neighborhood like the Village, the varied stock of buildings might seem drab, jumbled, even ugly. Jacobs pointed out that a mix of old and new buildings allows for people of different incomes to live together, and for businesses to start up with relatively little capital. Like Richard Florida, who was strongly influenced by her thought, she understood that low rents—particularly mixed among more upscale buildings—fostered new ventures among the young and the edgy. And, as she explains more thoroughly in her later books about the economies of cities, innovation and spinning-off of enterprises are necessary for economic growth and health. "Large swatches of construction built at one time are inherently inefficient for sheltering wide ranges of cultural, population and business diversity," she wrote. Even corner grocery stores have a hard time making a go of it if they must pay the kind of rents owners of new buildings expect. The space sometimes put aside for small stores in high-rise public housing is rarely used for convenience stores; the volume of business isn't large enough to cover the costs.

Density is extremely important, she wrote at a time when the big guns in urban planning were still traumatized by the very real health hazards posed by urban density when sewer systems weren't common and horses were the major source of transportation energy within cities. Lewis Mumford's *The City in History*, also published in 1961, cogently reviewed the development of cities around the world, but heaped scorn upon the idea that density can do anything other than foster disease and psychological misery. Garden cities and suburbs hold out much more promise for good living, he maintained.

At the time she was writing *Death and Life* Jane Jacobs seems to have agreed that there was something good to be said for the semi-bucolic life of the "real suburbs." She made a careful distinction between overcrowding and density: the former was what occurred when too many people lived in a single housing unit, but density was something quite different. Uncrowded but dense neighborhoods are ones that work, she wrote. "The tremendous gray belts of relatively low density that ring our cities, decaying and being deserted, or decaying and being overcrowded," are significant signals of the typical failure of low densities in big cities. Six dwellings per acre (fifteen per hectare) or less are fine for real suburbs, but between ten and twenty per acre (twenty-five to fifty per hectare) are "semi-suburbs," usually composed of detached or two-family houses on small plots, or of larger row houses on bigger lots. These densities are too low, she wrote, to contend with city problems and are destined to become gray areas "fit generally for nothing but trouble." The cut-off point for vibrant city life, she said, comes at about a hundred dwellings per acre, about 250 per hectare. (It should be noted that there are many ways of measuring density, including dwellings per hectare or acre, residents per hectare or acre, and residents or jobs per hectare or acre. This can be confusing—sometimes intentionally so, it seems.)

Greenwich Village at the time that Jacobs and her family lived there had 125 to 200 dwelling units per acre, with a wide variety of dwelling types—small single-family houses, two- or three-story apartment buildings, "elevator" apartments, and flats above shop space. This mixture kept the neighborhood from being standardized, and welcomed many different kinds of residents. The Jacobs' own home, a three-story building, had an empty shop space on the first floor when they moved in. The young family lived on the upper two floors as they renovated and remodeled the building. In the Ginger Press book, Jane says that eventually they had the kitchen across the front, the dining room in the middle, with the living room in back, opening onto a yard. In front was a tree which they planted in 1956. (A recent Google Earth satellite photo shows large trees on the sidewalk, as well as big trees filling the courtyard formed by the buildings fronting on Hudson and adjacent streets. The ground floor of 555 Hudson has been returned to commercial use, as City Cricket, an upscale children's store.)

A conversation that nine-year-old Ned had with a surveyor gave the first hint that the City of New York had plans to change the neighborhood radically. Sidewalks were going to be cut by ten feet (about three meters) to make way for more traffic lanes. The battle to save the sidewalks was the first that Jane Jacobs was involved in. The morning after her children told her about the city's plan—"We'd all noticed [the workers] making their chalk marks, but they wouldn't tell any of the grown-ups in the neighborhood what they were up to"—the Jacobs clan and friends got up a petition which a printer on the street printed for them. She said later that the fight was important for the bigger ones the neighborhood was soon be involved in: "People said 'We beat them on sidewalks, we'll beat them on this.'"

As Jacobs recounts it, the Hudson Street sidewalks were wide enough for children to play on and for grown-ups to loiter and chat, and still allow other pedestrians to pass by on their daily rounds. The neighborhood also had the short blocks that she said greatly aided the liveliness of an urban district. Long blocks, as laid out on the usual grid pattern, are "oppressive" and "boring." They also mean that neighborhood businesses are effectively limited to clients who live on the same street, since people prefer not to retrace their steps to get to a fruit stand or shoe repair shop in the middle of a long block on the other side. With frequent cross-streets, however, the neighborhood is opened up to foot traffic, which means the client basin is much deeper than one single street.

The section of Greenwich Village that the Jacobs lived in benefited from the fact that it was near the point where the several old grids laid out in the late eighteenth century met the grid established in 1811. It is easier to cut over a street or two when headed for the subway or other errands and there are several ways to walk home. To critics who say that more streets mean more surface to be paved over, she replied that the trade-off is worth it—and not that difficult to accomplish in cities where there is concern about deterioration of building stock. Far better to do a little demolition here and there of dilapidated houses or small factories and cut through short streets or use the space for small parks than to raze a whole neighborhood and replace the housing with all-of-a-kind high-rise blocks.

In Jane Jacobs' New York, however, little changes were not on the menu. Robert Moses, who was in charge of both parks and roads, was pushing highways in the 1950s, and massive rebuilding of the city on a Haussmannian scale. His idea was to use the road which ran through Washington Square Park as a feeder road between two major highway projects. The road at the time was "being used well below capacity" according to Moses, so he and his planners decided that it was perfectly logical to use it as the link between midtown Manhattan and what Jacobs called "a vast, yawning Radiant City and highway."

Moses had not counted on Jane and her friends. "Two daring women, Mrs. Shirley Hayes and Mrs. Edith Lyons," Jacobs wrote, were not only opposed to Moses' plans to widen the road through the park, but they also began to agitate for closing it to traffic entirely. Jacobs often said later that it takes at least three fights before a freeway project is killed, rather like a multi-headed dragon that must be slain again and again. The neighborhood group and their allies pushed Moses into a corner until finally he was reduced to shouting at a public meeting that "There is nobody against this—NOBODY, NOBODY, NOBODY, but a bunch of—a bunch of MOTHERS," whereupon he stormed out. In the end, "the mothers" not only stopped the freeway construction, they also succeeded in removing cars from the park.

Today real estate values in Greenwich Village have gone sky-high and even areas of Manhattan for which Jacobs had little hope, like Chelsea, are more than prospering. The Jacobses did not stick around to see this, though. They headed north to Canada, for reasons that had nothing directly to do with Robert Moses and his friends, but everything to do with politics. They emigrated because their two draft-age sons risked being inducted into the U.S. military and being forced to fight in Vietnam, a war the family did not agree with.

Toronto, the city they chose to move to, was younger than the city they were leaving, but like New York, had been laid out on a grid from the beginning.

York (as Toronto was originally called) in 1803, the year that New York had a population of about sixty-five thousand, and the entire island of Manhattan was being plotted. In British North America, concession roads were laid out 1.25 miles (two kilometers) apart, with the first concession usually aligned along a waterfront. In Toronto, Queen Street is the name for that first concession, with Bloor Street marking the second concession and St. Clair, the third.

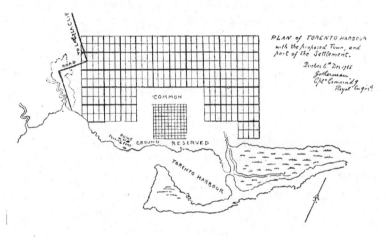

York (as Toronto was originally called) in 1803.

The Canadian city's basic rectangular grid continues today over much of the central area. A notable exception occurs around the system of ravines. Also, off-grid are two major thoroughfares which date to the very beginning of settlement in the region, Yonge Street and Dundas Street. Both were built in the 1790s, when John Graves Simcoe was the first lieutenant governor of Upper Canada, during the troubled times when the British were trying to consolidate their holdings in North America. Thirteen of Britain's North American colonies had just broken away during the American Revolutionary War, and France was in the throes of its own Revolution.

Yonge Street, named after Sir George Yonge, a British Secretary of War who never visited the continent, was designed to lead from the harbor at York to Lake Simcoe on the way to the upper Great Lakes. Work began in the dead of winter in 1794; that sounds like the very worst time to undertake a major construction project, but surveyor Augustus Jones of the Queen's Rangers preferred to work then because surveying was easier when the leaves weren't on the trees. The frozen ground also made it easier to haul cleared logs out of the way. The road the Rangers cut was twenty feet (just over six meters) wide; 200-acre (about 81-hectare) lots on either side were also surveyed. The first year they only got as far as Thornhill, about 30 kilometers (about 18 miles) north of the starting point (and not far from Vellore Park, which we'll visit later). Border tensions with the fledgling U.S. called the Rangers away and they did not return until 1796, when they cut through the bush for 433 days until they reached Lake Simcoe. Today Yonge runs straight as a die north past the first three concession roads, but then angles off to the east. Beyond that it makes very few deviations, despite the terrain which is cut by watercourses.

Dundas Street was also named after a British official, Henry Dundas, Viscount Melville, British Secretary of State for the Home Department. It follows the lay of the land much more closely, and so is more like the kind of road that developed in Europe over the centuries. Also begun in 1794, it was intended to link the settlement of York with Dundas, a town near the westernmost point of Lake Ontario, and at that time, a bustling port. Dundas begins south of the second concession road— now Bloor Street—but angles northward to cross it, and then continues westward and along the base of the Niagara Escarpment.

As Toronto grew, the grid continued to be the basis of development, but some of the big blocks in the central area were cut by small streets darting from one large road to another, thus avoiding the long blocks which Jane Jacobs criticized in the great New York plan. This is particularly true in working-class neighborhoods developed during the second half of the nineteenth century as the city industrialized and workers walked from neighborhoods like Cabbagetown to the mills and breweries in the Don Valley or to the docks and shipyards on the waterfront.

Jane Jacobs and her family moved to this comfortable house in the Annex district of Toronto after they left New York. In 2006, the year of her death, the goldenrod in the front yard was gorgeous.

The neighborhood that Jane Jacobs and her family settled in, the Annex, was also more or less laid out on a grid when it was planned in the 1890s. Just north of Bloor Street, it was intended to be home to professionals and to academics who would teach at the University of Toronto, just south of Bloor. While the Jacobs family initially rented on Spadina Avenue, a major thoroughfare, they soon bought on Albany Avenue. The house was a roomy three stories, a short walk from Bloor and its shops with a park, church and school a block in the other direction. The house and the neighborhood became the center of Jane's life for nearly forty years. When she died, the front yard was given over to wildflowers, and it is obvious that she loved making the most of its gardening possibilities. Her letters to her mother in the 1970s and '80s are full of references to what she's planting, to what is in bloom, to how the tomatoes are doing. She gives long accounts too, of her son's experiments with rooftop gardening, using sawdust instead of earth to cut down on weight, and rigging up watering systems with rain barrels and hoses run up the side of the house.

There is a certain irony in the happy life the Jacobses found in the Annex, because its density is about a 150 persons per hectare (about sixty per acre). Even though it is five times that of the thirty per hectare found in most suburbs, the density is at the lower limit of what Jane Jacobs advocated in *Death and Life* for a "lively" urban neighborhood. According to the criteria she gave there, the Annex falls in the "semi-suburb" category of ten to twenty dwellings per acre or between 145 and 190 residents per hectare. Neighborhoods with this kind of density "can be viable and safe if they are secluded from city life; for example if they lie toward the outer edges of a big city," she wrote in *Death and Life*. But "they will not generate city liveliness of public life—their populations are too thin—nor will they help maintain sidewalk safety."

The saving grace of the Annex may be that in addition to having a large number of single-family houses, some of which have been broken up into apartments, it also has a mixture of apartment block and commercial businesses along Bloor and to a lesser extent on Bathurst and other streets. The subway stations—Bathurst is on the next corner from the Jacobs' house—as well as other nearby transit links make it a neighborhood where people can come and go easily. People from outside come in to shop and study, while people who live there move around, traveling to work or school there or to other parts of the city. However, if Jane Jacobs changed her mind about what density was desirable in a city—and she certainly didn't mention doing so in her subsequent books—she never let up pressure for preserving a walkable, livable city. No sooner was the family installed on Albany Street than plans came to a head over the proposed Spadina expressway which would not only have pushed through the Annex, but also fundamentally changed downtown Toronto.

As she wrote in *The Globe and Mail* in 1969: "Up at Highway 401 we could see what Marshall McLuhan calls the launching pad, a big, confident interchange poised for imminent attack up on a wide swath of raw earth and for subsequent invasion of still unviolated ravine and pleasant community to the south. In the mind's eye, one could see the great trees and jolly Edwardian porches falling before the onslaught." She goes on to write that she and her family couldn't believe the freeway would actually be built. Expressways that have ripped through the urban tissue of many other cities have frequently made it harder to get around while removing many of the interesting places where one might want to go. It took several years of the Stop Spadina movement, but finally the Spadina expressway idea was abandoned. One of the ways Jane Jacobs celebrated was to take a bag full of maple and slippery elm seeds she'd raked up in her backyard on Albany Street and sow them in the land ripped bare in preparation for the expressway which wasn't built. Significantly, the slippery elm was a tree she'd saved from being chopped down when Dutch elm disease arrived in Toronto. "I feel it was one of my great accomplishments that the tree is saved," she said thirty years later.

Supposedly, Toronto was operating under a city plan which was designed for people, not automobiles. As "Proposals for a New Plan for Toronto," published in 1966 and designed for public discussion before the Toronto Planning Board, put it:

> A choice must now be made as to how this region will grow. Will it grow haphazardly with a continuously increasing reliance on automobiles, or can a pattern of orderly growth be established, with development focused on mass transit so that reliance on cars is reduced?
>
> If houses, shopping and industry are spread out over wide areas more travel will be needed, public transit will be uneconomic and people will be forced to use their cars to get around. Traffic congestion will be severe and life in the city will be under the tyranny of the automobile. This situation would be cause enough to question unlimited sprawl. But there are many other reasons. The greater the spread, the more people are immersed in it, divorced from the countryside and the city center alike. New highways and services have to be built through the existing city to accommodate the sprawling growth. This is difficult, costly and unsatisfactory; inevitably expedient decisions are made in response to urgent needs, resulting in a patch-work of compromises ...
>
> This fact is being recognized by the focusing of development around subway stations. In the region the equivalent of the subway would be high speed long distance mass transit train services, such as a commuter train system.

In some respects this planning effort was an attempt to compensate for the type of development that had been the norm in the 1950s, which saw Don Mills develop as the archetypal North American suburb (as we shall see later).

Eventually, Toronto made choices which kept it from following slavishly what was happening in most of the rest of North America. Among the victories for a more concentrated city is the way that Spadina Road eventually became the route for a new streetcar line which meshes effortlessly with the Bloor-Danforth subway line. Jane Jacobs and Spadina were by then closely linked in the public's mind. By then she also had become a beloved character. At her death in 2006 several essays celebrating her life mentioned how she would surge down an aisle at a public meeting in her later years, often brandishing her ear trumpet, the better to hear the discussion or the questions addressed to her. The portraits were loving, appreciative—and comic. She had become an icon, the archetypal outsider who had shaken things up. That a woman without the usual credentials stopped freeways and profoundly changed the discourse about cities in North America gave hope to people. For Canadians she was particularly precious because she had chosen the country over the colossus to the South, for all the right reasons, had made its biggest city her base and never stopped talking about how what was good about it should be saved.

But there was much more to her than her Raging Granny persona. In all she wrote eight books. Besides a memoir of an aunt, *A Schoolteacher in Old Alaska*, they can be divided into three categories: her groundbreaking book *The Death and Life* about what makes a city work for the people who live there; books about the role cities play as creators of wealth and motors of the economy, and philosophical works.

The economics books are less known to the general reader than *The Death and Life*, but *The Economy of Cities* and *Cities and the Wealth of Nations: Principles of Economic Life* found attentive readers among economists. Robert Lucas, Jr., who would win the Nobel Prize in Economics in 1995, started the ball rolling with a paper published in 1988 which pegged a major reason for differences in development among cities and regions to what came to be known as the "Jacobs externalities." These are the boosts that ideas, education and innovativeness give to an economy, the increases in human capital that result in better ways to do things and in new things themselves. Cities are the places where such exchanges take place, Jane Jacobs insisted, and Lucas agreed. As Lucas wrote "What are people paying Manhattan or downtown Chicago rents for, if not for being near other people?" Indeed, the importance of this human capital exchange explains much of the reason why cities continue to exist. Other economic factors, such as the cost of land, actually argue against the concentrations of people, industry, and commerce in cities because the players, thinking in purely conventional economic terms, should want to go to places where the land is cheaper, that is, in the middle of nowhere.

To some extent that happens on the edges of city regions, Jacobs acknowledged in *Cities and the Wealth of Nations*. In it, she expands the argumentation about the importance of cities and their hinterlands as places where diverse things are made, first to replace goods that have previously been imported, and then to export new modifications and completely new inventions. The incorporation of surrounding settlements into a city is a normal event in its growth. The city's influence on the countryside around it is also felt through improvements in agriculture which reflect the increase in innovations and technology that come from a city's effervescence, she asserts. She gives as an example of the transformation of agriculture in California from grain and cattle production at the beginning of the twentieth century to fruits and vegetables. Refrigeration and canning, both technological developments born in the city, opened up new possibilities for food conservation, and therefore new products to export could be developed.

In between these books which solidly addressed economic questions, Jane Jacobs took on the thorny problem of Quebec separatism in the Massey Lectures, the series which the Canadian Broadcasting Corporation commissions from a prominent thinker each year. The question of Quebec and Canadian unity probably was not on the minds of the organizers when they asked her to do the job in 1979, but, always original, she turned to one of the greatest challenges of her adopted country. She begins by saying that as an outsider she has developed an affinity for Canada, but admits that she has only an intellectual understanding of what Quebeckers must feel for Quebec. Then she goes on to do an analysis of the growth of Montreal as the center of French-language industry and culture in Canada. Her conclusion? It would make a great deal of sense for Quebec, with Montreal as its metropolis, to go it alone, given the great need of cities to have control over their own development in order to create what she called export-replacing industry.

The Question of Separatism made waves in Quebec, but elsewhere it was considered more or less a digression. Montreal writer Robin Philpott won a rare interview with her in 2005, when she was both struggling to finish her last book and waging a war against health problems, because he wanted to talk about Quebec; she said that no one had asked for her thoughts on the subject in a long while. Here as concretely as any place else Jacobs underscores the importance of cities as incubators for innovation, diversity, and wealth.

The next two books still are deeply concerned about cities, but in them Jane Jacobs takes a flyer at philosophy. In *Systems of Survival: A Dialogue on the Moral Foundations of Commerce and Politics* and *The Nature of Economies* she is obviously inspired by the form of the Platonic dialogue, as well as the imagined conversations she said she had from her childhood onward with the great thinkers of the world.

In *Systems of Survival* she brings together a group of friends, including Armbruster, a retired book publisher who bears a resemblance to Jason Epstein, Jane Jacobs' editor at Random House whom she thanks for his interest and faith in her ideas several times in her books. Armbruster convenes a symposium (in the Greek sense of a meeting for talk and eating) in order to discuss something that has been bothering him: the moral decline found in some corners of society while in others we blithely entrust our fortune and lives to strangers everyday. What does this mean?, he asks his friends. What is going on here?

Jane Jacobs apparently loved these kinds of meetings over food; she said they were a way to build community by breaking bread together or "commensality." One of the first winners of the Jane Jacobs Prize, which is designed to celebrate Toronto's "original, unsung heroes" in fact went to Roberto Martella, a restaurateur whose Grano was the scene of many such gatherings.

What Jacobs portrays in *Systems of Survival* is supposed to be the edited transcript of a tape made over several such lengthy and leisurely talks. How well it succeeds as an engaging, understandable meditation on moral systems is debatable. The reviews were mixed. *The New York*

Times had two, one from Christopher Lehmann-Haupt which summarized the arguments and concluded by saying that the book would go up on the shelf with Jacobs' other works "to be consulted from time to time for their quirky and original views and the way they cut through to the essence of things." Alan Wolfe was more critical, saying that she presented evidence to fit her analytical framework, which is "not especially original" anyway. Furthermore, "real people do not live ethical lives by following the precepts of intellectual syndromes," Wolfe wrote. "Their worlds are built from experience up, not from abstractions down. The younger Jane Jacobs drove this point home. The more mature one seems to have forgotten it."

The book's basic argument is that there are two moral systems operating in human society, and only two. One can be called "commercial" or "Trader" and may be derived from the mechanisms that humans have developed since they began exchanging what they made, caught, or grew. Jacobs and her imaginary friends call the other system the "Guardian" system. It is an outgrowth of the "taking" way of life which humans lived exclusively before they developed the social and production skills needed for producing and then trading pottery or excess food or tools or clothing. Each system—perhaps too neatly to be believable—boils down to fifteen precepts. The Trader system is built on shunning force, coming to voluntary agreements, practicing honesty, and investing for productive purposes, for example. The Guardian system, in contrast, requires shunning trading, exerting prowess, exacting obedience, and dispensing largesse, among other things.

Jane Jacobs seems to think the Trader system makes more sense in our current life, but she also allows Armbruster's friends to point out the good points of the Guardian system: it works well in military organizations, in religion, and in some aspects of government, for example. A nation has a responsibility to do such things as enforce contracts, go after crime, and safeguard its people's health, she says. The last requirement, by the way, should lay to rest any thought that she would be in favor of a chaotic, privatized health system: providing universal health care to a country's citizens is tinkering with the system, she would argue, not corrupting it.

But confusing the systems, mixing up principles from both of them, can lead to monsters. She mentions the Mafia as an example of combining a Trader framework with a Guardian ethos in the interest of crime. Implicit in the discussion is the damage that can be wrought when Guardian precepts like "dispense largesse" are applied in contexts where they shouldn't be. What she means by "largesse" includes providing "magnificence" as gifts, usually in reward for good Guardian behavior such as obedience. In later years she seems not to have publicly applied this analysis to political life, but to read critiques of post-9/11 political behavior in the United States by such commentators as the economist Paul Krugman, who cites her in his own groundbreaking *Geography and Trade*, is to see how powerful this framework is. The cronyism of the George W. Bush administration, the largesse it dispenses to its friends through defense contracts, and the soft landing it provides for its figureheads who fail (Krugman mentions several who got cushy jobs in his *The Conscience of a Liberal*) all speak to a Guardian system run amok with the taxpayers' funds. (In contrast, Krugman emphasizes the good record of Franklin Delano Roosevelt's New Deal which handed around a lot of money in the 1930s and '40s, to admirable effect.)

This is not to say that Jane Jacobs is completely against the Guardian system. She has Armbruster's friends argue whether this means that artists are better supported by it; obviously largesse in the form of the grand realizations of cathedrals and courts have produced great work and provided much employment for artists. But she does not make any of them comment on a kind of largesse that she railed against for most of her life: the projects which are supposed to make cities more beautiful, like the dreams of Haussmann or Robert Moses. In interviews she argued that architects for the slum-clearing projects of the 1960s behaved as if they were part of the Guardian system. She says that photographers from slum renewal agencies went out of their way to portray as unhealthy the districts their agencies wanted to tear down. They actually falsified the pictures they were taking, she says, in a textbook example of the Guardian's principle, "Deceive for the sake of the task."

As she explained to an interviewer for *Reason* magazine, when the two systems get confused "they get corrupt, and they get skewed in non-functional ways." Urban renewal policy-setters are "really guardians, they're really territorial administrators, but they have provided monetary incentives for the private sector to do things it wouldn't do otherwise, and that's a mess."

Keeping in mind the dangers of mixing the two systems of behavior is important in thinking about cities and our world, but so is recognizing that cities and the economy are actually closely integrated elements in nature. Jacobs expands on this idea in a second Platonic symposium, *The Nature of Economies*, in which Armbruster and his niece Kate have a another series of discussions around meals. Natural systems have built-in feedback systems, and so do economies and life in cities, Jacobs writes. If these systems reinforce what has been going on, they can become what we commonly call vicious circles. Her friends mention the tragedy of over-fishing, where smaller catches incite fishermen to fish more, not less, thus making the situation worse. But her friends also talk about what happens when roads become congested, creating traffic jams and longer travel times. One response would be to decide that too much reliance was being placed on the road system, and to switch to public transit and rail to reduce highway traffic. Another would be to build more roads, but this actually encourages more use of cars and trucks so that pressure will mount to widen existing streets and to build even more new ones. "The result of enormous expenditures and effort has been that cars still crawl at some twelve miles an hour during lengthening rush hours," says Hiram, one of Armbruster's friends.

The need for cars in low-density suburban areas is a feedback loop which intersects the road congestion one, Hiram says. Because the distances traveled are greater per number of passengers, the transit routes are expensive, which encourages cutting back on transit which in turn makes cars even more necessary, with the result that even people who can't really afford them, have to have cars.

Deciding whether to put public money in more roads or in public transit is one of these situations where either choice will have effects that aren't anticipated. Switching from horse-drawn vehicles to cars, for example, was a societal decision—a bifurcation, Jacobs calls it—which had two marvelous consequences: it got rid of the mountains of manure produced by horses, and reduced pressure on agricultural land to produce food for the animals. But what replaced horses and what that technological shift encouraged, headed us off in other, even more problematic directions.

Jacobs adds that when one of the disastrous vicious circles develops it will usually eventually crash under the weight of its consequences.

But if it is sustained by infusions of largesse—in the case of the fishery, by loans to buy more fishing equipment, and in the case of roads, by pouring millions into highway construction—the damage may go on and on because it is artificially sustained by outside forces.

She comes down hard on the automobile/roads/suburban sprawl cycle in her last book *Dark Age Ahead*. Not only do many of the attempts to improve traffic flow for particular areas—she cites the approaches to the Verrazano Narrows Bridge that links Brooklyn and Staten Island—often destroy the very neighborhoods they're supposed to help, but many of the methods used have absolutely no effect. She compares how fast you can walk in downtown Toronto to how cars must crawl along, respecting the "no turn," "one way" and other rules. There is no research that shows this accomplishes very much, she says, adding that in the background of the traffic engineers' plans, "I see little boys with toy cars happily murmuring, 'Zoom, Zoom, Zoom.'"

Take that, Baron Haussmann, she might have been saying.

All through her life, she returned again and again to the pedestrian as the center of the city. As she told *Reason* magazine, the lively heart of a real town or city is always where two or more well-used pedestrian thoroughfares meet. It is the corner that is important, the foot traffic which makes the place an interesting place. Many people don't see this, and she notes that her first book got violently different reactions because there are "foot people and car people." The former, she wrote in a later introduction to the Modern Library edition of *Death and Life*, found that the book corroborated their own experience of the city, because they saw it on foot. Car people reacted quite differently—and negatively.

Let us return to the hot early summer night in Greenwich Village, though, because returning to the real world is what Jane Jacobs, despite her delight in imaginary conversations, counseled everyone to do. You can't understand what you're seeing without looking at it closely, she said again and again.

And what are the two women talking about this typical, sticky New York evening? About Jane Jacobs and the way she and her family finally have had enough of what was going on in the U.S., New York, and the West Village. A couple of months earlier, last April when spring was in the air and summer was a distant rumor, Jane had been arrested during a hearing on a resurrected Lower Manhattan Expressway plan. She was alleged to have urged "more than ten persons to the stage and [to] engage in violence," and to have destroyed minutes of the meeting and to have damaged a stenographic machine. The charge: second-degree riot and criminal mischief, carrying a possible sentence of four years. Nonsense, she protested when she pleaded not guilty. She and her friends were only involved in a peaceful march down the aisle of the meeting hall and across the stage. "The inference seems to be," she told *The New York Times*, "that anybody who criticizes a state program is going to get it in the neck." In the end, the charges were reduced to a fine and friends rallied around to raise money for the legal costs she incurred. By then the Jacobs family had moved to Toronto.

On this hot night, though, the news of the move has just begun to circulate widely. Bob was taking an architectural job working on the design for a new hospital in the Canadian city. The Jacobs sons would not have to worry about the draft, and Jane, who'd also been arrested for demonstrating against the Vietnam War, would not have to worry about her tax money going to pay for a conflict that she profoundly disapproved of.

How like the Jacobs, her neighbors might have said as the twilight deepens this hot night, how typical of those great walkers and marchers, to finally vote with their feet!

In the next few chapters we'll follow Jane Jacobs' example and take some walks ourselves to see what the real world is like today. We'll examine what walking is like now, what it says about cities and their future, and why we need to make them walkable. The first stop will be back in Paris, but we'll also revisit Toronto and points west.

THREE

Walking the Walk II
Perambulations in the Real World

CHAPTER 5

Rue Mouffetard, Paris

From Before the Romans to Haussmann's Day

TOWARD THE END OF MAY, the sun sets late on the rue Mouffetard. The street runs southward from near the top of Montagne Ste-Geneviève, and the slanting rays of the setting sun illuminate the tops of the buildings on the hill. With the work day over, slim women trailing tartan-covered shopping carts on wheels stop at the Franprix grocery to pick up bottled water and dish soap. They may buy a small roast chicken and browned potatoes at one shop opening onto the narrow street, then choose a perfect Chanterais melon, a handful of fresh, crisp salad greens and some white asparagus at the open-air greengrocer halfway down the hill toward the Église St-Médard. As they turn off the street toward the century-old apartment blocks on the rue Claude-Bernard or head home to a restored eighteenth-century *hôtel particulier* on an even narrower lane, they pass young people sitting on terraces, sipping beer or lemonade while they wait to join friends for dinner in a café a little later.

This is, to some minds, the quintessential Parisian experience: the present-day city where walking is still a favorite way of getting around, where it is easy to walk along paths first trod literally thousands of years ago. Looking at this neighborhood closely one can also see how a city changes over time. The past, both recent and ancient, is just a scratch away beneath the surface. Despite its quaintness, this street is not a Disney version. The big tourist attractions of Notre Dame and the Louvre are both a half-hour or so away by foot. The *grands ensembles*—the Le Corbusier-inspired apartment towers built to house the deserving poor in the last half of the twentieth century—are so distant as to be invisible. There has been some destruction of old buildings in the neighborhood, but the rue Mouffetard continues as a narrow, slightly meandering route taken by Parisians since long before the settlement on the Seine took Paris as its name.

The street itself is part of an old road that led toward Rome, beginning at the site of one of the oldest bridges on the Seine, the Petit-Pont. There was a bridge here when Julius Caesar marched through Gaul: the torching of the five-arch wooden structure is mentioned in his *Commentaries*. This suggests that the road existed for a considerable time before, but no one knows for sure. Built and rebuilt many times since, the current bridge begins steps away from the grand courtyard of Notre Dame Cathedral on the Île de la Cité.

From there, the original road turned a little east and south and began to wend its way around Montagne Ste-Geneviève, the hill which dominates the Left Bank. Following what is now the rue Lagrange, it turned onto what is now the rue de la Montagne Ste-Geneviève. There it climbed the slope to the east side of St-Étienne du Mont Church, skirted the top of the hill along what is now rue Descartes, and then headed down the hill and onward toward, eventually, Italy. Today the rue Mouffetard as a street name begins at the point where the wall built by Philip Auguste ended: the Place de la Contrescarpe to the west marks its edge. At times the Place, just outside the authority of the city for centuries, attracted protesters against the established order. Both the ribald sixteenth-century priest-writer Rabelais and the fifteenth-century poet François Villon made the Pomme de pin tavern on the Place their headquarters. At the end of the slope, Mouffetard becomes the avenue des Gobelins, one of Haussmann's broad boulevards, and continues toward the Place d'Italie, another of Haussmann's creations.

Tonight, standing at the top of the rue Mouffetard and watching the nicely dressed women run their errands, the young dark-haired men keeping the fruit and vegetable stands, and the young couple wheeling a toddler in a stroller down the street, we can garner an idea of how pleasant it can be to live in a really walkable city. There are a few vehicles on the upper reaches of the street, but this is not a road to drive along merely to get there from here. To move around in this neighborhood, one walks, or maybe rides a bike or roller blades. It is less of a stretch of the imagination to see the crowds of people who walked along this street over the centuries than it is to conjure up the smells of a hundred years ago.

The air on this pleasant evening is scented by the last of the

Narrow rue Mouffetard follows part of a road leading south. It goes back more than two thousand years, but hums with activity today.

chestnut blossoms which hang on trees planted in hidden courtyards. A hint of gasoline fumes floats by, accompanied by the faint noise of traffic on Haussmann's boulevards. The mix is not offensive, and very far from the atmosphere that weighed down the neighborhood for literally centuries when the smells from the tanning and other industries at the south end of the street poisoned the air. The street's very name is linked to the odors. While some sources say that it is a corruption of the Romans' name for a hill a bit farther on, Mons Cetardus, local residents long ago linked it to the word for something stinking, *moffette*, a word given by the French to that furry little white-striped black animal they encountered in North America, the skunk or *moufette*.

Ernest Hemingway rented an apartment just off the rue Mouffetard in the 1920s, and complained about the smell. Industry had begun to move out by then but the narrow buildings were not hooked up to Paris's sewers (another Haussmannian project which nevertheless did not cover the entire city). The buildings' *toilettes turques* or squat toilets, one per floor usually, emptied into cesspools at the bottom which were pumped out into horse-drawn collection wagons at night. "In summer time, with all the windows open, we would hear the pumping and the odor was very strong," he recalled with his hallmark understatement in *A Moveable Feast*.

But at one point this part of Paris was as bucolic as any freshly-minted North American suburb circa 1950. The Bièvre, a river whose source was 33 kilometers (23 miles) away near Versailles and whose name comes from the Latin word for beaver, *biber*, wound through a valley it had cut between the Montagne Ste-Geneviève and the Butte aux Cailles to the east, entering the Seine near the Pont Petit. What was to become the rue Mouffetard crossed the stream on a bridge at the bottom of the slope close by the present Église St-Médard.

The current church building dates to no earlier than the sixteenth century, but there was a village and church here for more than a thousand years. A reference to the church's existence is found in accounts of the laying of the first stone at Notre Dame in 1163, while other texts suggest that an earlier building was burned during the Norman invasions three hundred years earlier. Much of the land on this side of the Seine was held by religious orders who used the property as farms and refuges away from the city. The Bièvre itself was first diverted in the twelfth century by the Abbaye St-Victor, which dug a canal to irrigate its gardens. The canal, which sent part of the Bièvre's flow into the Seine where the Pont Austerlitz now is, was just the beginning of the stream's transformation.

Water was the main source of power for machinery until the Industrial Revolution, and also was the easiest way to get rid of whatever wasn't wanted. The fact that the bridge across the stream near the Église St-Médard, was called the Pont aux Tripes suggests that at least one abattoir began operating nearby early on. Records from medieval times make it clear that dyeing textiles and working with hides were trades practiced in the village of St-Médard which grew up near the church. The men, women and children who worked in these trades did not have to travel far to get to work. Workshops were in the courtyard behind a house or just around the corner.

A reminder of this period lies a short way beyond the narrow confines of the rue Mouffetard. If we cross the end of the open-air market at the bottom of the street, we find ourselves facing a tree-studded open space, gorgeous in this season with the lavender blooms of Pawlonia

The open-air market stalls and the shops that open onto rue Mouffetard attract thousands on weekends.

trees. The Église St-Médard sits to our left while the prospect of a wide boulevard opens before us to the south. Follow it, and we soon come to the workshops of the famed Gobelins tapestry-makers from which Haussmann took the name for this grand wide street, the avenue des Gobelins. The factory, set up by a family of dyers in the middle of the sixteenth century, was bought a hundred years later by Louis XIV to furnish his sumptuous residences with tapestries and upholstery. Production continued almost continuously until the French Revolution, and in the nineteenth century a rebuilt factory began to turn out carpets. During this long period the Bièvre was used as a handy sewer in which to dump industrial wastes. Add that to the detritus from leather work which continued even though the sources of hides were now further away, and the result was a watercourse that stank, surrounded by piles of refuse that also smelled. No wonder the people in the neighborhood called the street Mouffetard, so tightly linked to the idea of stench.

Just as the stream was profoundly changed over the centuries, so were the people who worked in the industries of the neighborhood. In 1724 when rue Mouffetard and the village of St-Médard, along with other neighborhoods outside the previous city walls, were incorporated into Paris, eyebrows were raised because of the "uncivilized" behavior of the new citizens of the city. Certainly those who lived near the growing industries of the Bièvre were poorer than the opinion-makers of Paris, but even people building on the slopes of the hill during the eighteenth century were often struggling. An example is the lawyer who built his house and garden on the street paralleling the rue Mouffetard, the rue Tournefort. The building's central staircase survives, graced by a fine wrought-iron balustrade, but the garden has long since been built on: the lawyer lost land and building when he went bankrupt in the mid-1700s. This is the part of the neighborhood which Honoré Balzac called "the ugliest quarter of Paris, and, it may be added, the least known" at the beginning of his novel *Père Goriot*, which starts in one of the houses on rue Tournefort (then called rue Neuve Ste-Geneviève.) The even more densely populated, and *populaire* in the French sense of working-class, sections further down the hill became famous for their incendiary spirit during the French Revolution in the 1790s. Later the men of the Mouffe' were on the barricades during all uprisings of the nineteenth century—1830, 1834, 1848 and 1871. Indeed, the bloody insurrection of the Commune began in March 1871 with an attack on the Republican Guard armory on the rue Mouffetard.

But that lay in the future when Haussmann began working with Napoléon III to remake Paris. While the first big projects were concentrated on the Right Bank, from the beginning Haussmann wanted to do away the tangle of streets on the Left Bank. He knew parts of it well, since the route he had taken during his days as a law student led him through the blocks just west of the Pont Petit. From there he turned up the rue de la Montagne Ste-Geneviève to his college near the top of the hill. In his memoirs he writes scathingly of the district, particularly "the miserable little Place St-Michel" through which ran all the waste water from many streets, and at the bottom of which was, "like a discordance, the sign of the celebrated perfumer Cardin."

The major changes on the Left Bank came in increments. Haussmann's first projects rearranged the area where he had walked as a student. First came the boulevard St-Michel, which would also form the southern extension of the grand crossroads at the center of Paris. Then came the completion of the rue des Écoles, which connected major educational institutions that could previously only be reached by circuitous routes. La Mouffe' and its surroundings were only affected by the second wave of transformation. While both Haussmann and Napoléon III officially downplayed the strategic value of making wide roadways where troops could march easily, it seems no accident that this second wave created new, broader streets which circled the Montagne Ste-Geneviève and its student population. The rue Monge on the east and north, and the combined arc of the rues Gay-Lussac and Claude-Bernard begin well to the west of the rue Mouffetard and then circle south to meet near the old course of the Bièvre, now buried and transformed into part of the sewer system.

Destruction of existing buildings to create the new streets removed many working-class dwellings, shops, and small businesses. The families of workers were forced to move further out, to neighborhoods having even fewer services than the most neglected parts of central Paris. As Zola's tragic heroine Gervaise remarks about Glacière, the neighborhood south and west of the industrial area centered on the Bièvre, the suburbs were "way to hell and gone … where there's always mud up to your knees." All over Paris as Haussmann's streets were cut through, the poor and the working poor had to move outward, toward Belleville, Menilmont, Montmartre—neighborhoods beyond the old *mur d'octroi* where building codes were often non-existent. In some cases the newly-developed areas were closer to new factories being built where land was cheaper and less encumbered than in central Paris. Workers from Belleville could walk down the hill to the engine works near the Gare de l'Est, for example. But, in a pattern that would continue until the present, many displaced workers had to travel longer and longer distances. Zola's Gervaise can get from the Goutte d'Or to the Glacière by omnibus, the horse-drawn carriage that was Paris's first successful public transport, but it takes so long that she only does it once. There is no question of living there and working on the other side of Paris no matter how attractive a job might be.

When trouble came in 1871, unhappy industrial workers led the revolt which followed the defeat of the French by the Prussians, the death of Napoléon III, and the disgracing of Haussmann because of the cost of his grand projects. They held the hilltops surrounding central Paris during days of ferocious fighting when many symbols of the powers Haussmann had favored were torched. The Palace of the Tuileries and the Hôtel de Ville were among them. In the latter it appeared that all copies of Napoléon III's map showing which streets were to be constructed went up in smoke. Sixty years later, a copy that someone had given to Wilhelm II of Germany was found, just one of many ironies in the long conflict between Germany and France.

But when the conflicts of the 1870s were settled, construction went on within the outlines set up by Haussmann and Napoléon III. Paris welcomed the world to large international exhibitions in 1889 and 1900. The City of Light gleamed with electricity before almost any other, its fashions were the talk of the world, and its music and art set the tone for the twentieth century.

All the while, life continued on the rue Mouffetard and in the neighborhood to the south. More than once the narrow street was threatened with redevelopment. Just a couple of blocks away, the quaintly named rue de l'Épée-de-Bois (Street of the Wooden Sword) had most of its old buildings razed in the middle of the twentieth century, while here and there on rue Mouffetard itself modern construction—a school, and the new library, for example—was undertaken. Rather than destroying the cachet of the street, however, the more recent buildings say, this place is still in the game, it isn't a museum, things change, the neighborhood adapts, but we aren't going to do away in a frenzy of demolition with what good has come down to us from the past.

So the area is studded with reminders of what happened here. Plaques on corners giving the names of streets also frequently give the dates of the person after whom the streets are named—rue Jean Calvin (1509-1564) runs into the rue Mouffetard about halfway down the hill, for example. Other plaques indicate where luminaries of the past lived, like Prosper Merimée, author of *Carmen*, on rue Tournefort. Since we are walking down Mouffetard in early May, and May 8 is a holiday celebrating the end of World War II, there also will be flowers hanging from plaques in sad memory of the deportation of Jewish residents, like the one on the rue Vauquelin marking the school from which a group of girls was taken.

Other monuments to the vigor of this neighborhood are more elusive than bricks, stone and mortar, but convey vividly what life was like here in the past. Take the series of photos shot by pioneer photographer Eugène Atget. One made about 1880 shows a flower seller, aged no more than thirteen or fourteen, his hair brushed, his boots either too big or protecting feet that on a puppy would suggest a size at maturity approaching the gigantic.

Eighty years later Henri Cartier-Bresson took a photo (sadly no longer available for reproduction) of another Mouffetard boy. Shot on a warm afternoon in 1954, it shows him carrying two bottles of wine, cradling one in each arm. The cork in the one on the right sticks a little above the mouth of the bottle: this is not a *grand cru*, but *vin ordinaire* from a neighborhood shop. A grin spreads across the boy's face as he steps cockily forward. He looks mischievous and pleased with himself, and it is easy to imagine that a second after the shutter clicks he will toss a cheeky remark in the direction of the photographer. As it is, he is frozen in time with his scabby knees showing below his shorts, his feet sockless in his sandals and his undershirt sticking out where his nearly-outgrown sweater is too short to cover his belly.

The wine shops on rue Mouffetard today are more up-market than the one where the boy shopped. The Franprix supermarket has the cheap wine; the specialty shops cater to those who know a bit about *apellation*

Young flower seller on rue Mouffetard, c. 1880.

d'origine contrôlée and vintage years, and who can pay more. But walking down rue Mouffetard is as much a pleasure now as it was then. At the bottom, we can stop on the Square Maubert, *prendre un verre* at one of the cafés perhaps, and look out on the ensemble of buildings which still bear the mark of Haussmann's plans for this city.

While this neighborhood was for centuries outside Paris, first as the country holdings of religious orders, and then as one of the first industrial suburbs, today it displays the best of urban life, Paris-style. The five- and six-story buildings which line the wide Haussmannian streets coming together here—rue Monge, rue Claude-Bernard and avenue des Gobelins—offer a captivating harmony of design. Looking at the light-colored stone façades and the horizontal lines marking each story with windows rhythmically repeating the same lines, one may be tempted to credit the Baron with having had a vision of unifying the city through architectural details. That would be wrong: his plans only built on a handful of regulations governing building heights, allowable building materials, and details like the horizontal lines, most of which actually had been in place for nearly a hundred years when the reconstruction began. The result of this traditional multi-story building style is development capable of housing thousands of people in a relatively confined space, while allowing a lively street life amid a built environment which combines aesthetic harmony with dignified commonality.

The shops on rue Monge have windows full of signs and merchandise-—telephone cards, bargains on household wares, photocopies and publicity for internet servers. The very hodge-podge quality of what they offer shows the neighborhood's vitality. One can buy almost anything here, and if one needs to leave the quarter, all one has to do is hop a bus—three lines run down Claude-Bernard, another half-dozen ply the other two streets, or take a Métro: three stops on three different lines within a ten-minute walk. The density of the population, the advantages of living where many people come together, are apparent. Why would anyone want to live in any other place?

But of course, not everyone can. Ask one of the men who so politely serve the slim ladies shopping for supper on the rue Mouffetard where they live, and the answer is likely to be, "Not around here. Too expensive for ordinary working folk these days." The boy with his wine bottles, or his equivalent, is more likely to be living in one of the Paris suburbs, perhaps in a big apartment block, in one of the *grands ensembles*. His Paris will not be the walkable one of the rue Mouffetard; his suburban life will be the antithesis of suburban life in North America.

[CHAPTER 6]

Greenland Drive, Toronto
A Prototype of North America's Suburbs

During a good part of the twentieth century, a life in the suburbs was the goal for millions of North Americans. Particularly after World War II, single- family houses set on individual lots couldn't be built fast enough to keep up with demand. This sunny winter midday we are walking down the pleasant streets of Don Mills, Canada's original Garden City built on former farmland northeast of Toronto, to see what a collective dream looks like.

Along the edge of the roadway—there are no sidewalks in this section—footprints of people and their pets pockmark the snow. The only people out on foot now are two thirty-something women who appear to be headed for Greenland School, the elementary school which will let out for lunch in a couple of minutes, and an elderly power walker who strides along energetically, pumping his arms and raising his knees high as if he recently and reluctantly gave up jogging. Now more than fifty years old, some of the houses we will walk past are sheltering a third or fourth generation of suburbanites who like the relative closeness of downtown Toronto and the peaceful winding streets of this model town.

Before Don Mills there had been earlier experiments with planned suburbs in Canada and the United States. Inspired by Ebenezer Howard and Patrick Geddes, who argued that the ills of the Industrial Revolution could be cured by building new towns beyond the edge of existing cities, the Garden City movement was the philosophical underpinning for an attempt to transform cities that was very different from Haussmann's approach. The first English New Town was begun in 1904, but the

The corner of Deepwood Crescent and Greenland Road in the
bucolic Toronto suburb of Don Mills.

concept remained a dream until after World War II even though it influenced many urban planners.

At its purest, a Garden City New Town was supposed to be a self-sufficient community of sixty thousand or so, with enough jobs, housing, recreational opportunities, and services that its residents wouldn't have to deal with larger cities. Because of their size and because the idea was developed before the rise of the automobile, classic Garden Cities would probably have been walkable cities, even though their design resonated with a powerful current of anti-city thinking in the late nineteenth century. Frederic Law Olmsted—himself designer of Riverdale, an early suburb outside Chicago which was based on the idea of railroad links to the center city—advocated the "ruralizing of all our urban population and the urbanizing of our rustic population." That was part of his motivation for fighting to substitute graceful, curving streets for Manhattan's enormous grid in the years after he and Calvert Vaux planned Central Park. Had he won that battle, much of Manhattan would have taken quite a different form than the one which pleased Jane Jacobs so much.

However, separating industry and business from residential areas was a major motivation behind New York's adoption of one of North America's first land-use, or zoning, regulations. The 1916 law also set up rules for building skyscrapers that regulated the intense high-rise construction boom of the post-World War I years and remained in force for nearly fifty years. Zoned, largely residential communities sprang up on the edge of cities from the beginning of the twentieth century onward.

Radburn, a New Jersey suburb built in the 1920s, is often credited as being the North American model of this type of development, but the Town of Mount Royal near Montreal preceded it. Originally called Model City, the Town of Mount Royal was promoted by the Canadian Northern Railway in the first decades of the twentieth century. Partly to finance building a new terminus in downtown Montreal, the railway quietly bought up more than 3,200 hectares (8,000 acres) of farmland north of Montreal's mountain, also known as Mount Royal. Profits from residential and industrial development would pay for the downtown showplace and a railroad tunnel underneath Mount Royal.

It was an ambitious project. The new town's layout was "inspired by Washington, D.C., the municipality's promotional material states.

As in the U.S. capital, streets converge on a central circle where civic buildings, churches and a business district cluster around a park with the commuter train station just steps away. But timing was bad for the endeavor. Construction of the tunnel took a year, with completion coming in 1913 shortly before the beginning of World War I. Delays during the war meant that the first trains did not run until 1918. Then the railroad company went into bankruptcy; it was acquired by Canadian National Railways. Some residential construction in the Town of Mount Royal was completed in the 1920s, but during the Depression of the 1930s relatively few houses were built. It wasn't until the 1940s that the Town really took off. Today the Town of Mount Royal (known as Ville Mont-Royal in French) is still served by a commuter rail station near the town center, but twenty-eight trains pass each day, compared to forty-four at the height of rail commuting in the 1940s.

Don Mills was begun just as the Town of Mount Royal was finally succeeding. In area it is smaller than the Town of Mount Royal, but through a combination of better timing and astute planning, it took only ten years to create a community housing more than twenty-five thousand people and a commercial and industrial district.

The area is isolated from the urban center by two branches of the Don River, and by railroad tracks heading north from the city. The Don is one of two main rivers flowing south from the Oak Ridge Moraine toward Lake Ontario. Since the end of the last Ice Age, they and their tributaries have carried silt and sand from the moraine to form the spit of land which shelters Toronto's harbor. The ravines the streams flow through are the signal characteristic of Toronto's landscape, even though today someone traveling across the city may be unaware of their existence. Many of the streams have been dammed, covered over or even, like Garrison Creek and Taddle Creek, turned into sewers as the Bièvre was in Paris. Major roads cross the streams and their ravines on high bridges, and the subway tunnels under them. It is to his credit that the father of Don Mills, the tycoon E. P. Taylor, insisted that the new development conserve the wild beauty of the ravines and integrate the remnants of the ancient landscape into the suburban fabric.

Apparently, Taylor, who had irons in many fires, did not originally think of building a major Garden City project when he began quietly buying farmland in 1947. The word was that he wanted to expand his brewery operation—his Argus Corporation was the principle partner in O'Keefe brewery, which was the world's biggest—with new plant and housing for workers. Don Mills Road was a winding, two-lane thoroughfare; Lawrence Avenue, the major east-west route, was similar. But if all went well, one could drive from the crossroads to downtown Toronto in half an hour.

Taylor may not have realized what he was undertaking when he bought the land, but by the time it was amassed, it was clear that he was aiming for something more than an ordinary housing development whose only purpose would be to make a quick buck. His timing was excellent because the moment had come to change the way North Americans lived and respond to an enormous pent-up demand for decent housing.

In her last book *Dark Age Ahead* Jane Jacobs tells how she and her sister—like many others—doubled up in order to pay rent during the Depression, while during World War II when wages were higher she and her husband took in two young women doing war work to help pay the rising rent. By the end of the war, "the affordable housing shortage…was so acute, and evictions were so alarmingly common, that the shortage had become a crisis," she writes. The problem had at least three possible solutions: court-enforced rent controls, slum clearance and subsidized housing projects, and long-term government-guaranteed mortgages for new housing. All three were tried, but it was the last which substantially changed the housing stock in North America. (In Great Britain where the housing shortage was even more acute because not only had little been built in the 1930s, but much was destroyed during the War, a combination of apartment blocks built by government in existing cities as social housing and suburban new towns was the option adopted.)

The team that Taylor brought together to plan and build Don Mills included architects and planners who admired Ebenezer Howard's Garden City ideas. It was clear from the beginning, however, that the Don Mills new town would not be self-sufficient as Howard proposed, but, like almost all North American suburban development, closely linked to the larger city. Nevertheless, Taylor's team intended to include a variety of housing types and opportunities for jobs for the people who lived in them. The lead planner was Macklin Hancock, a twenty-seven-year-old architect who had never undertaken a major project. He divided the terrain into four quadrants with each one designed as a neighborhood centered on an elementary school. A commercial center, the Don Mills Center, stood near the crossroads; it would become both the shopping area and the community heart. Low-rise apartment houses were built within walking distance of the center, but the quadrants were filled with single-family houses set on winding streets where through traffic from the outside world had no reason to travel.

Most of the couples who bought the houses had steady incomes, but were neither wealthy nor poor. The really well-off wanted to build their own houses, while working-class families could not afford the $13,000 or so the houses went for in the 1950s, even with the help of government-insured loans. In general, the people who worked in the industry and services in the Don Mills industrial park couldn't afford to buy in Don Mills. Finding workers for businesses in suburban developments is a problem that shows up again and again where planning regulations prevent mixes of housing types and insist on putting commercial and industrial uses away from residential areas.

Buyers were attracted to Don Mills not only by the quality of the housing construction (Taylor set very high standards, going so far as to prohibit blue shingles because he didn't like them), but also because many of the natural advantages of the setting were preserved. For example, Taylor insisted that agreements with the school district on ceding school sites include the provision that no trees be cut down except for those actually growing where the school was to be constructed. Nuances of topography were also respected: the rise and fall of the land wasn't bulldozed away to make lots easier to build on. Originally the streets did not have paved drainage channels at their edges, so that rain and snow melt-water could be absorbed into the ground, thereby recharging the water table. Most, if not all, of the ditches are paved now, but there is still active concern about the wooded areas and the development's edges which descend into the ravines.

The first quadrant to be developed lies northwest of the intersection of Don Mills Road and Lawrence Avenue; the first family moved into a house on Jacelyn Crescent in 1954. At the time, Don Mills was overwhelmingly white and middle-class. Best-selling writer Lawrence

Frank Lloyd Wright's prairie houses, like Robie House in the Chicago suburb of Hyde Park, strived for an almost mystical relation with the land, and had a big impact on North American suburban housing design.

Houses, like these low-slung houses in Don Mills set on lots large enough for a garden and trees, were the post-World War II suburban ideal.

Hill, his brother and sister, were the only children of color in the neighborhood when they were growing up. In his memoir *Black Berry Sweet Juice: Growing up Black and White in Canada*, Hill explains that his father, an African-American who had grown disgusted with racial politics in the U.S., and his mother, a fair-skinned woman whose family had come to the United States from Northern Europe, left the U.S. because they wanted to raise their children in a less racially-charged atmosphere. The choice had advantages and disadvantages, Hill writes, because being so "different" from the other children presented challenges.

Times have changed, though, and Greenland School is far from a white-bread school today. About two hundred students in junior kindergarten through Grade 5 come from nearly thirty different language groups; 20 percent of the pupils weren't born in Canada.

Greenland, right up there on the corner where the little yellow school bus is waiting, was founded in 1955, and moved into its own building in January 1956. Now it also houses a daycare center. It is right next to St. Mark's Presbyterian Church. Across the street is Don Mills Middle School, and a few steps away sits Don Mills Collegiate Institute. The idea was that school would be just a short walk or bike ride away from home, and that the looping, quiet streets would be great for children at play. The lots—18.3 by 30.5 meters (60 by 100 feet) was the standard—are big enough for gardens and games, but the houses as originally built were on the small side by early twenty-first-century standards. Although two hundred different designs were eventually constructed, the basic house had three bedrooms (some two-bedroom ones were planned but never built because the local planning department objected) and a carport, but not a garage. They came with basements (construction without one in Toronto's climate is almost unthinkable) but elaborate game rooms, home offices, and a bedroom for each child were things of the future. Most of the designs were strongly influenced by the current of residential architecture inspired by Frank Lloyd Wright's prairie houses. Low and frequently long, Wright's houses were intended to have an almost mystical relation to the land on which they were built. By the time Don Mills was under construction, the style had been watered down considerably, but much of the suburb's architectural tone comes from Wright's legacy.

Greenland Road runs into Donway East, a curving street that connects with Don Mills Road. This is the apartment area of the development: more than half of the housing units were apartments, a fact that is often forgotten when the image of Don Mills is conjured up. The density of dwelling units in this section is higher than for Don Mills as a whole, which is about 9.6 per hectare, or 4.9 per acre, about half that suggested by New Urbanism and much lower than Jane Jacobs recommended.

There is no skimping on green space. As we walk on this sunny day, off to the left we can see the beginning of a pedestrian trail which runs along the back of several houses, widening out and eventually becoming Moccasin Trail Park. In this season of bare trees the blue sky shines through branches and the drifts of snow sparkle in the sunlight. But we continue straight ahead, encountering a few more people on foot, older women bundled up against the cold pulling grocery carts behind them, a grandfatherly-type pushing a fancy stroller, a young woman with a backpack. They're headed for the shopping center across the street. As Jeanetta Vickers, who moved in during the 1960s, told *Eye Weekly* in 2007, "It's very handy here. I don't drive, but I can walk everywhere. There are a lot of seniors here who don't need a car."

And that is the telling difference between Don Mills and the suburban developments which followed it. While it was expected that most families buying here would have a car, things were laid out so that walking was possible within the development. The day of the two or more vehicle family was far in the future. Few women with children worked outside their homes, and getting around on foot was factored into the equation from the beginning.

Although Don Mills' design aimed to integrate jobs, most of the men probably drove to work in the center of Toronto. The commute wasn't bad at the beginning, but as more farmland around Toronto was turned into housing developments, traffic volume increased rapidly. When the Don Valley Parkway opened in the mid-1960s, congestion was reduced for a while. The expressway had two lanes in each direction, and was part of a grand plan that would have seen several expressways cutting into the downtown Toronto core including the Spadina route that Jane Jacobs helped fight successfully. But traffic improvement on the DVP was only temporary; two lanes had to be added in the 1980s by removing the grassy median strip and replacing it with a concrete barrier. In the classic "if you build it, they will come" scenario, the highway was soon flooded with traffic again, becoming anything but an expressway during rush hours. Nevertheless, the private automobile remains the means of transportation of choice for most Don Mills residents even though buses do connect with subway stations two or three kilometers (one or two miles) away.

Don Mills inspired developments all over the country. Few of these tried to integrate jobs and apartment housing, and most were not as successful in combining nature with housing. The more usual pattern was for one set of developers to lay out housing while another built the local and regional shopping districts. Planning authorities—city, county, regional, state, or provincial—applied zoning regulations and saw that services like sewers and water were provided. Rarely did one authority take charge of all aspects of development. Of the thousands of developments built during the last half of the twentieth century only about a hundred and fifty tried to construct a whole, integrated community. Three of these were studied by Harvard planner Ann Forsyth at the turn of the twenty-first century to see which had adhered most closely to the principles of what is often called the planned unit development. She looked at Columbia in Maryland, at Irvine, California, and at The Woodlands, north of Houston, Texas.

In many respects the thinking behind the communities Forsyth studied is similar to the planning precepts underlying Don Mills. These developments began with larger acreages, however; the biggest, the Irvine Ranch, consists of about 90,000 acres (about 36,400 hectares) in the valley south of Los Angeles. When fully built, their populations will be much bigger too, up to four hundred thousand people. All three contain large nature reserves as well as significant employment opportunities, with more jobs than households by the late 1990s. Like Hancock, Taylor and their team in Don Mills, the planners of all three new towns used a neighborhood of between three and ten thousand people as the basic unit of development. An elementary school and neighborhood shops provide a core for each neighborhood; regional recreation and shopping facilities serve several similar-sized neighborhoods.

Children may have been initially expected to walk to the school, but otherwise there is nothing that encouraged walkability. Public transit was rarely integrated into the development. To live in it, a family needs at least one car, or maybe more, while to buy a house in one of these communities today means one very good wage, if not two. As for the vaunted advantages of the free, outdoor life children were supposed to live in this kind of suburb, kids today often spend more time in after-school activities than playing on the wide quiet cul-de-sacs their houses sit on. In many suburbs the only person walking is the nanny.

But, on this day in Don Mills, it still is possible to run a few errands on foot. Obviously some shoppers do it every day, despite the cold and snow. We stop at the light, waiting to cross to the shopping center. The cars whiz pass; traffic is not so heavy that speed is reduced. That will likely come later in the afternoon, though, when people start to make their way home.

Quick, the light is green. Cross while the crossing's good.

CHAPTER 7

Avenue Vincent-Auriol, Paris
The City After Haussmann

ANOTHER NOONTIME, another season, another country.

At the southern end of avenue des Gobelins lies the Place d'Italie. Look north and we can see the boulevard losing itself at the base of rue Mouffetard with the dome of the Panthéon on the top of the Montagne Ste-Geneviève rising behind. This is another of the grand views that Haussmann's transformation gave to Paris—the backdrops for daily life that surprise and please the visitor.

The Place d'Italie once marked the edge of the *murs d'octroi,* the boundary at which duty was collected on products entering the city. There were two collection pavilions here, both stormed in 1789 as the Revolution began, but remaining in place long after the area to the south became part of the city of Paris in 1860. The Place in its current configuration dates from the turn of the twentieth century, and was intended to remind one of the Place d'Étoile on the Right Bank.

Three lines of Métro cross underneath. The entrances to the stations are on the periphery, but if we want to take a closer look at the central open space itself, we turn right and follow the far edge of the five-lane traffic circle which surrounds the Place. At the one point where we can safely cross to the green space in the middle, we wait until traffic stops at the light. Then we saunter across to a real island in the busy city, passing concentric rings of trees and bushes to the circular pond in the middle. A fountain sends a great jet of water into the air. Several large trees shade the wide gravel walkway. As we stroll around, there are late spring flowers to inspect, a little statue of a naked boy to admire, a few other promenaders to spy on. The peacefulness of the Place today contrasts with its reputation as the site for demonstrations in time of

Place d'Italie. The tallest building in Paris was once planned for its southern edge.

labor, student or ethnic strife, and also with the swirling traffic. In classic Haussmannian style, the circularity of the Place is set off by six streets leading from it like spokes of a wheel. When the Place was laid out, the roadway would have been filled with horse-drawn vehicles carrying goods and the gentry. Now this route, along which men and women have walked for more than two millennia, seems to belong to an entirely different universe than the one where walking was the norm for most people.

But zooming traffic this late morning is neither as heavy as it would have been earlier in the day, nor as it will be in the late afternoon when drivers use the broad street for access to the Périphérique, the autoroute which circles central Paris, following the outline of the Enceinte de Thiers. The fortifications, built in 1861, marked, and still mark, the political limits of the city of Paris. Long before the walls were pulled down in 1919, they had been removed from the line of the city's defenses. Actually their military worthlessness was shown ten years after their completion when the Germans were able to besiege Paris for 132 days during the Prussian War of 1870. But even before then, the grassy slopes of the outside of the wall became a place where people displaced by Haussmann's projects constructed their own shelters. By 1912 two-thirds of the land was covered by the shacks of the *fortifs*, and as late as 1926, 42,300 squatters were counted living in a jumble of constructions like those that can be found today on the outskirts of Dar-es-Salaam or São Paulo.

For years Parisians and their leaders discussed what should be done with the land formerly just outside the walls. During the 1930s several lots were sold to private developers, and nearly thirty-nine thousand units of social housing were built in seven-story buildings which housed about a hundred and twenty thousand people. In 1943, in the midst of the German occupation during World War II, the collaborationist Vichy government considered making a broad pedestrian-friendly boulevard along the line of the fortifications. The plan called for sidewalks 3 meters (about 10 feet) wide, and 8 meters (about 26 feet) of planted space down the middle, rivaling the Champs Elysées, but much longer than that legendary promenade since the new one would encircle the city. After the war the plan was forgotten, in part because of its association with the government of occupation, but also because winds of change were affecting the thinking of urban planners in France as well as elsewhere in the world.

Haussmann's Paris, after all, had been the city of the future, the City of Light and progress. That legacy was still present, but in many ways France at the middle of the twentieth century found itself with big problems and many questions about where it was going. There was agitation for independence in its former colonies, thousands of people were ill-housed and had been for decades, and, perhaps worse for the country's *amour propre*, the spotlight of world attention had shifted to North America where New York, unscathed by war, became for many the capital of the world. That the East Side of Manhattan was chosen to be the site of the United Nations was a fact not lost on the nation that had welcomed the League of Nations headquarters after the First World War.

As Jane Jacobs pointed out, the French did not listen to Le Corbusier when he proposed leveling the center of Paris so that cars could circulate freely there. But what she didn't mention is that many of his ideas were adopted at the edges of French cities. The thought of tall buildings where light would stream into apartments and healthy living was supposedly guaranteed, as well as the principle of separating residential from other uses, seemed extremely desirable in post-war Paris. Le Corbusier's formula of big apartment blocks set in green space was translated into a number of developments, some designed for the working poor, but others supposed to attract the well-heeled young who would, it was thought, want modern housing not far from the center of the city. Paris, French leaders assumed, was going to have to embrace the automobile in order to fulfill its twentieth-century destiny. It would have to build more skyscrapers to make up for the long period during the war when nothing was built and to alleviate overcrowded housing.

One of the areas targeted for reconstruction lies to the south and east of the Place d'Italie, between the avenue d'Italie and the curving course of the Seine. This is the 13th arrondissement. The Mairie, the district's administrative offices, are housed in the grand Haussmannian building on the northwest corner where the avenue des Gobelins joins the Place. When the space between the *mur d'octroi* and the Enceinte de Thiers was annexed to Paris, Haussmann reorganized the system of districts: the old arrondissements on the Right Bank and Left Bank became, more or less, arrondissements 1 to 8, counting in a clockwise direction from a mythic center of Paris located somewhere near the grand carrefour of the boulevards Sébastopol and Rivoli. The territory further from the historic center became arrondissements 9 to 20, again counting in a clockwise direction: that's why the 13th arrondissement is directly south of the 5th. It may seem illogical to those accustomed to cities laid out on grids where numbering goes from north to south or vice versa. But like many things French, what appears whimsical is very carefully reasoned.

The 13th had several *îlots insalubres*, large groupings of buildings and streets considered to be slums because of their high density and high tuberculosis incidence; TB rates were used all over the developed world as a shorthand indicator of neighborhood health. In *The Death and Life,* Jane Jacobs even trotted out low TB rates in North Boston to prove the area was not a slum even though Boston city planners considered it one and were planning to tear it down in the 1950s and 1960s. The use of tuberculosis as an indicator for slum conditions lost much of its relevance when TB rates plummeted because of effective drug therapy in the 1960s, and because it became clear that the relation to housing was only tangential.

The "slums" of the 13th were concentrated around the industrial area to the east of the avenue d'Italie into which railroad tracks run. The Gare d'Austerlitz fronts on the Seine with its switching yards extending south. A smaller rail line, the Ligne de petite ceinture, circles just inside the old Enceinte de Thiers, connecting the major railroad stations of the city. For decades the area hummed with factories; cars were manufactured, sugar refined, and fruits and vegetables processed, among other things. The housing, some of it in large multistory buildings which followed the old Parisian plan of stores and small workshops on the first floors with lodgings above, was a short walk from jobs in the centuries-old pattern. But as the post-World War II period progressed, much of this industry moved farther away from the center and deeper into the suburbs where there was room to build modern plants. What remained were large expanses of decaying industrial buildings as well as housing that appeared substandard, even if the people who lived in it weren't getting TB as much as they might have in the past.

It was a time of political change, too. France, as it had done several

Avenue Vincent-Auriol passes over the railroad tracks leading south from
the Gare d'Austerlitz in the heart of the 13th arrondissement, once an
industrial suburb.

times since the Revolution at the end of the eighteenth century, broke
with its political past once again at the end of the 1950s. A new
constitution was adopted, giving the popularly-elected president of the
Republic far more powers than previously. Charles de Gaulle, who had
championed the new constitution, was elected president in 1958, bringing
with him a group of thinkers who wanted to return France to the
forefront in the domain of ideas and development. This was the period
of great reconstruction of British cities, and the beginning of Le
Corbusier-inspired changes in North American city centers. Paris had
to strut its stuff too, but of course in a way that was particularly French.

It was another Haussmannian era, some urban critics said, and the
term had either a favorable or a disparaging spin, depending on who
was speaking. The 13th arrondissement was to be one of the showcases
of a great modernist project. Another would be La Défense, a second
city center west of the city limits on another curve in the Seine. When
critics protested that the high towers proposed were a betrayal of the
beloved Paris full of five- and six-story buildings which Haussmann's
regulations had encouraged, the planners argued that the new projects
were only creating a new standard silhouette for the city. Just as the

four-story Place des Vosges, constructed in the sixteenth century, set the tone for France until the late eighteenth century when the five- and six-story buildings became the norm, the new towers would provide this new, rebuilt Paris with a uniform skyline. But as happened many places elsewhere in the world, the big projects were not the success expected.

As we stand in the Place d'Italie, we can look across to the modernist shopping center, Italie2, on the southeast side. It is on the northern fringe of this redevelopment area, called Italie XIII. Plans proposed widening the avenue d'Italie so it could serve to funnel traffic into the center of Paris; De Gaulle's successor Georges Pompidou declared, "The city must adapt to the automobile." Pedestrians would only be able to cross it in tunnels or above-ground passageways, while high-rises would provide a "signal" that drivers were entering the center of a revitalized Paris.

As these plans were being made, the debate about what to do with the vacant land of the old fortifications, the Enceinte de Thiers, was concluded. More housing and a few sports facilities would be built, but mostly the area would be given over to the automobile. The Périphérique, the expressway ringing the city, was opened in the late 1960s. Somewhat ironically, in 1967 an automobile manufacturer closed its plant a little north of the Périphérique and east of the avenue d'Italie. The newly available space was earmarked for a shopping complex, while a forest of towers went up in various parts of the neighborhood. Some of these were disasters before they were even constructed and by the mid-1970s, after the first petroleum crisis sparked reconsideration of reliance on the automobile, the project was abandoned. The French government ended up paying 470 million francs (about 100 million euros) to a developer whose permits it ultimately had to revoke. A sort of twentieth-century version of the *campaniles* found in many Italian cities now stands where the tallest building in Paris was to have been built. Constructed of steel and glass, the tower features thin bars like uplifted arms thrusting out of its structure.

The nearby Olympiades was one of the most ambitious parts of the redevelopment scheme, and in the end, probably the most successful. These four tall towers set above old warehouse space on the Ligne de petite ceinture were supposed to attract the young and relatively well-heeled when they opened in the early 1970s. Built on the parcels of land without any relation to the existing street layout, a hallmark of urbanist thinking of the time, they didn't attract the intended clientèle and in fact were basically empty for a couple of years. It was only at the end of the U.S.-Vietnam War with the arrival of thousands of refugees from South-East Asia that the towers found tenants. Sometimes families doubled up in order to afford the rather high rents, but in the last three decades the new arrivals have prospered and saved the Olympiades from becoming another high-rise disaster. The neighborhood is now known as Chinatown, and the shops at street level are as lively as those found in high-rise developments in Singapore or Hong Kong.

But that's a good twenty-minute walk away from the Place d'Italie. This noontime, we'll head off to the east along the avenue Vincent Auriol. The divided boulevard, named after a president of the Fourth Republic, has a park-like strip down the center as broad as the traffic lanes. On the south side trees line the street, and many of the buildings have the panache that seems to go with mature trees and well tended public green space. There are a few cafés. At one, a couple sits on a terrace with glasses of wine in front of them, waiting perhaps to enjoy an early lunch. It's too early to stop, though, and so we continue, pleased that trees on this side offer shade as the temperature on this late spring day begins to rise.

The other side is a different story. Here buildings come right to the sidewalk for many blocks. The sun bounces off the pale gray concrete, the slightly darker stone. One of the things that makes Paris such a beautiful city is the way it glitters in the light. The building stone used during Haussmann's time and earlier is of a pale color, and regulations that date from his era require that façades be cleaned at least every ten years. The requirement was not enforced during the first part of the twentieth century, but when the problems with urban redevelopment led to a major shift in ideas about how the city should evolve in the 1970s, the government began to require regular cleaning. The result is a city that in many places lives up to its reputation as the City of Light, even if that was initially a reference to the early adoption of electricity for street lighting.

The change in attitude in the mid-1970s toward grand projects had more effect in other parts of Paris than along this boulevard. A major result of the realization that historic Paris was unique and worth preserving was the abandonment of all ideas of changes in the traffic pattern of the central arrondissements and a concentration on conserving the historical context of the city. On the Right Bank, the Marais, where *îlot insalubre* No. 3 inspired plans for completely razing the historic section, was saved and rehabilitated, from the inside out, in effect. Much work was done on sewer, water, and electric infrastructure, but the basic outline of the walkable city, laid out six hundred years ago, remained.

Around the avenue Vincent Auriol some high-rise apartments from the 1960s and 1970s have settled into an uneasy relation with the elements of the city dating from the time when the neighborhood was an industrial suburb. We can see them as we walk along: small stores tucked into old buildings or in the first floors of bigger blocks, with signs in Arabic as well as French, the big Casino grocery store which advertises parking in the rear, a couple of cafés filling up with workers as the noon hour moves on. Because the walking has made us hungry, we stop and have a baguette sandwich at one of them before we continue sauntering along. Buses roar along the road, and down the middle of the boulevard the Métro runs on elevated tracks; it plunges below ground just east of the Place d'Italie. There is graffiti on the walls of a high-rise apartment complex to the south. The elevated train lines cast shadows and the noise of the traffic echoes against the hard surfaces of the buildings where there is less foliage to muffle the noise.

The 13th is far from the picturesque Paris of the central arrondissements, and here we will not find the same sort of care lavished on safeguarding the detail of buildings. Just to the north of the avenue Vincent Auriol, however, lie the extensive grounds and well-preserved buildings of the Pitié-Salpetrière hospital. Begun in the seventeenth century on the site of an old gunpowder factory (salpêtre, or potassium nitrate, is a constituent of gunpowder), the hospital at first was a sort of hostel for the poor of Paris, but over the centuries it has become an internationally recognized medical institution. You can enter the 37-hectare (15-acre) compound from avenue Vincent-Auriol, but because of the way the complex is laid out, it effectively turns its back on its less elegant southern neighbors.

East of the hospital the avenue crosses the railroad on a bridge from which idle warehouses can be seen through the chain link fence which keeps interlopers out of the railroad yards. On the far side, a few of the Haussmann-era buildings which once housed workers remain, giving a taste of what the neighborhood must have been like for much of the twentieth century when it was an industrial suburb. There may be trees planted in a few back courtyards, or so aerial shots of the neighborhood suggest, but this stretch of the street is not terribly inviting. The atmosphere beyond the current limits of the city of Paris in the more recent industrial suburbs is even more depressing, however.

Suburbs do not mean the same thing in France, or in much of the rest of Europe, that they do in North America. Owning a house on a lot, however modest, has been something that most North Americans have aspired to for generations. Movement to the suburbs in France as well as Germany and some other European countries has been quite different; rather than choosing to move to the edges, in general people were forced to do so. Dissatisfaction with living conditions has been endemic in French suburbs from the time that Haussmann began clearing the working class out of central Paris. In the 1870s the stalwarts of the Commune held off the forces of order from the hills which were the fringes of the suburbs then, Montmartre and Belleville. In the mid-twentieth century the so-called "Red Suburbs" repeatedly elected Communist city councils. Fear of political foment in the suburbs motivated many politicians in the 1950s and 1960s to call for more and better housing for the working class; the catch phrase was that "bad housing leads to Communism."

In one of those philosophical flights aimed at regularizing and systematizing the world that are the glory and the despair of France, it was decided that the *cité jardin* on the edge of Paris and other French cities would overcome "the former disorder" of earlier urban planning. These "garden cities" were nothing like those proposed by Ebenezer Howard, despite the similarity in name, but took their inspiration directly from Le Corbusier. With few exceptions, they boiled down to housing developments remarkably like the high-rise projects which failed so dismally in the U.S.—towers set in green space with no regard for the idea of street life and little concern about public transportation. In the period between 1954 and 1974, two hundred thousand new dwellings of this kind were built inside Paris and as many or more in the surrounding areas. As Bernard Marchand notes in his work on the modern history of Paris, these apartments worked reasonably well for young families who were upwardly mobile. They were often better than the lodging the families had had previously, and, buoyed by post-war optimism, the families expected to move on to something even better. Marchand quotes a survey which showed that two-thirds of the people applying for apartments really dreamed of having a single-family house. Some people did prosper and moved to larger quarters. As the fabric of France, like that of other European nations, began to change with immigration from former colonies and elsewhere, these first residents were frequently replaced by immigrants.

The projects—the largest of which are also called *grands ensembles*—today have reputations as bad as those of New York and Chicago thirty years ago. While some of them were built with recreational facilities, most had none. Even worse, employment opportunities were not considered, nor were ways to link the developments to the greater city. (Paris, it should be added, has three "new towns" more or less on the British model in the metropolitan area, where train transportation is much better, and where rents and house prices attracted a wealthier clientele able to demand better services.) In the fall of 2005 many of the poorer suburbs exploded in three weeks of violence. The precipitating incident—three boys being chased by the police were electrocuted when they hid in a transformer installation—took place 15 kilometers (about 9 miles) northeast of Paris in the bucolic-sounding Clichy-sous-Bois. A village at the edge of a large forest reserve, the town became the site of several *grands ensembles* housing projects in the 1960s. A direct highway connecting the town to the industrial development around the Charles de Gaulle airport and Marne-la-Vallée, the new town to the south, was supposed to be built, but wasn't. Clichy-sous-Bois was left with more than six thousand units of public housing, but little opportunity for employment in the immediate area. It was a situation far too common around Paris, as well as around other French cities.

Before the dust settled in November 2005, more than nine thousand vehicles had been burned, and nearly three thousand young people had been arrested. The political repercussions were still being felt two years later when Nicolas Sarkozy, who as minister of the interior had taken a hard line on the troubles, was elected president of the Republic, in part because of the image of decisiveness that he gained. But anyone who had been following French film was unlikely to have been surprised at what happened in the banlieues. The grand winner at the Cannes Film Festival in 1996 was *La Haine* (Hate), a story of three young men from the projects who are struggling to make it in a Paris where they don't fit in at all. It begins with a voice-over telling the story of a man falling from one of the project towers, and saying as he passes each floor, "So far so good." It's only when the bottom is reached that the damage is done.

Here on the avenue Vincent Auriol we are far from Clichy-sous-Bois, but the building which stood at No. 20 has become something of a symbol of the malaise which comes from pushing the poor to the edges of society, both literally and figuratively. On the night of August 17, 2006 a fire of suspicious nature broke out there, whooshing up the central staircase and killing seventeen people, including fourteen children. All of them were immigrants or the children of immigrants from West Africa, legally in France, and living in a building which belonged to a French government agency. The housing, in fact, had been a sort of safe haven. A group of a hundred and one families had been evicted in the early 1990s from old workers' housing in the neighborhood that was to be torn down to build the new national library headquarters, and their plight and dignified comportment won them much public support. No. 20 avenue Vincent Auriol, which from photos looks as if it were much like thousands of other Haussmann-tradition Parisian buildings, was supposed to be only a short stop for them on the road to decent, publicly-supported housing. Some work on the building was done, repairs to the roof and foundation in particular, but when it came time to move the families out while more extensive renovations were undertaken, no substitute housing could be found because no one wanted to rent to such large families of black people. The 2006 fire and the underlying situation became the subject of a hit song by the rapper Médine, and investigations into the causes of both the fire and the plight of the families have continued into mid-2008. At this point plans are in the works to build a new structure on the site with twenty-seven units of social housing and a daycare center, but construction hasn't begun. On the wall of the building next door a large cross scrawled by a graffiti artist guards a big empty hole in the ground where No. 20 once stood.

The rest of the neighborhood is changing rapidly as part of a large redevelopment plan, which urbanists hope will not encounter the same problems that Italie XIII did. Called Paris Rive Gauche, it concentrates on industrial land which is no longer being used. French government offices have gone in south and west of the railroad tracks where factories and warehouses once stood. The Grands Moulins, built along the Seine between 1919 and 1924 and which milled flour for the famous Parisian baguettes for more than sixty years, have recently been gutted and refurbished in order to house a campus of the Université de Paris. Nearby, refrigerated warehouses, also no longer used by industry, have been claimed by artists, with their vast spaces turned into galleries and ateliers as Les Frigos.

Back on Vincent Auriol, the burnished metal and concrete structure on the corner at No. 22-24 now houses a restaurant/bar/club called Djoon. Far from being the kind of bistro or local watering hole you might find in a working-class *quartier,* Djoon features large windows looking out at new construction under way and music that comes from as far afield as Chicago. "*Très loft new yorkais,*" one review put it.

Much of the multiple railroad tracks will soon be covered, more housing catering to different income groups is under construction, and more industrial buildings will find new vocations. The four towers of the Bibliothèque François Mitterrand of the Bibliothèque nationale are nearby too. Opened in 1996, the complex symbolizes the dynamism of French intellectual life, its long heritage of ideas, and also the problems that arise when a nation tries to wrestle the past into a framework dictated by the future.

Critics of the Très Grand Bibliothèque are many: professional archivists and librarians despair over the systems set up to cover windows in the towers, and thus to protect aging, and precious, books and manuscripts from light. Getting access to its resources can be complicated and cumbersome, particularly if the computer system is not functioning properly, as it apparently did frequently in the first months. The grand pavilion around which the towers are placed is windy, which makes using it as a place to enjoy views of the Seine not pleasant when the weather is cool. Similarly the sun on hot days glares off the pale wooden planking which covers the courtyard and dances off the many windows of the towers, increasing the heat. But it is worth walking around to take the measure of the place before descending the conveyor- belt-like

The site of No. 20, avenue Vincent-Auriol where seventeen immigrants died in a suspcious fire.

The Bibliothèque François-Mitterand of the Bibliothèque nationale is the cornerstone of the Paris Rive Gauche development.

sidewalk to the entrance at the exhibition and reception level. A small forest of trees and bushes grows in this central rectangle, invisible until we're right beside it. That some of the plantings required special bracing against the wind, while the pedestrian surfaces are very slippery in wet weather, has prompted much criticism, and some laughter.

When making a judgment on the building complex, though, it is probably good to remember that the Eiffel Tower was virulently criticized when it was built, that the Georges Pompidou Museum was shunned, and that I. M. Pei's glass pyramid at the Louvre was considered by many to be a travesty. Neverthless all have become a part of the city's mythology. The big terrace of the library may be a ringside seat for observing changes which presage Paris becoming a beacon which points the way toward how cities in the twenty-first century should be organized.

The broad steps leading down from the library toward the edge of the Seine are steep, but at the river's edge we find two new features of Parisian life. The first is a swimming pool floating in the Seine itself, filled with purified water from the great river and providing recreation for the masses; it is not accidental that it is named after Josephine Baker, the African-American singer and dancer who was the toast of Paris in the 1920s and '30s.

The second is the new footbridge across the Seine named after Simone de Beauvoir. It is part of an effort to undo the damage wrought by those powers in the late twentieth century who forgot that men and women were made to walk, and tried to adapt the city to the automobile. There are now three other bridges dedicated to cyclists and pedestrians. That means slightly more than 10 percent of the thirty-seven Seine crossings don't cater to motor vehicles. The proportion isn't great, but it does point in the direction that Paris is going: away from the private automobile and toward a sustainable, walkable city.

By 2020, the city aims to cut automobile traffic volume by 40 percent compared with that of (the year) 2000. Lest that sound like the wishful thinking surrounding greenhouse gas reduction targets many governments talk about but do little to realize, the current administration in Paris points with pride to the fact that between 2001 and 2005, automobile traffic actually declined by 15 percent. The idea is to increase constraints on cars systematically, while at the same time making

The footbridge across the Seine named after Simone de Beauvoir, and which leads to Parc Bercy and Bercy Village.

making it easier to use other means of transportation—Métro, bus, bicycle or foot.

Certainly, as the afternoon is ending and we walk out over the river with its barge traffic and its pleasure boats, it is easy to be seduced by the delights of a city which has returned to appreciating the human scale of travel by foot. On the other side of the Seine lies the new Parc Bercy, a gorgeous green space filled with gardens and places to enjoy nature. Just beyond the park, Bercy Village is being developed as a complex where very expensive housing sits beside subsidized units and where businesses and services offer places to work and shop to neighborhood residents. Well served by Métro and buses, this walkable neighborhood bursts with life all day long and well into the evening. It is one modern development that Jane Jacobs would probably love.

On Sunday the expressway lanes along the Seine in the central arrondissements will be free of cars—another highly popular measure instituted in the last few years—and people will walk, bike and scooter from place to place. How they get to work on Monday—a growing number use noisy motorbikes—is another question, but the fact that the city is expanding its public transportation network at least means that people have a number of choices as to how to get around.

As do we: if our feet are tired we can retrace our steps to the avenue Vincent Auriol and take the Métro to where we want to spend the evening. Paris is not perfect, but it certainly is better than most other cities.

[CHAPTER 8]

Vellore Park Road, Vaughan, Ontario
Taking Cues from Jane Jacobs
but Getting It Wrong

A FALL AFTERNOON north of Toronto and the mission is to get some milk, bread, and a few other things for friends who've just moved into their new home. The house is full of boxes that haven't been unpacked yet, although the beds upstairs have been assembled and made up with fresh sheets. The table in the kitchen is cleared, and the contents of two boxes marked "pots and pans" and "dishes" have been stowed in cabinets. At the moment the proud owners are off picking up the kids at their elementary school, taking the car.

We're going to have to walk in this new suburb which demonstrates some of the best and the worst aspects of current North American suburban development.

If this were the Annex where Jane Jacobs lived, or even Don Mills, the job would be easily accomplished. We'd walk out the door and turn toward the shopping street or the shopping center. True, in Don Mills the walk might be a kilometer or more, but because the suburb was planned at a time when families had only one car and most women stayed home, it is relatively compact, with shopping in the middle. The streets wind around, but the network of footpaths that are part of the development's nature plan also allow cutting through blocks and along backyards to make walking more direct.

But here in a neighborhood so new that the houses don't even show up on Google satellite photos, the undertaking is much harder.

Construction in the Vellore Park district of the City of Vaughan, north of Toronto, started in the winter of 2006-2007. In the 1990s the city had laid out the parameters for development in Block 33, one of the old land divisions in this formerly agricultural area. At the time the urban planning world was buzzing with talk of the New Urbanism, which was touted as the wave of the future. Taking their cue from Jane Jacobs, who famously included no illustrations in her *Death and Life* because readers were supposed to find examples in their own environments, the husband-and-wife team of Andrés Duany and Elizabeth Plater-Zyberk looked around their own pleasant Victorian neighborhood in New Haven, Connecticut in an attempt to figure out what made it work so well. By 1982 their ideas had evolved enough to plan Seaside, originally a funky beach community where walking was supposed to be as convenient and pleasurable as driving. They elaborated several principles, which were dubbed the New Urbanism and which aimed at completely changing the way new suburban development was undertaken. Instead of miles and miles of sprawl, New Urbanism favors compact neighborhoods with shopping, schools and parks close by, less than half a mile (somewhat less than a kilometer) in most cases. Mixed residential types should be encouraged, and allowance should be made for one separate unit on the back of each lot for a workshop, office or independent apartment to rent out, or for elderly parents or adult children. Public transit and a neighborhood center are essentials in this kind of development which aims for densities much higher than the usual suburban sprawl.

The current of thought has become so persuasive that the Greater Toronto Area now has seventeen areas deemed to be New Urbanist communities, more than any other city in North America. The City of Markham even engaged Duany to plan its Cornell district along New Urbanist lines. While the City of Vaughan did not go that far, two of its development areas, Vellore Park and Carrville, were originally designed and zoned so that developers could produce New Urbanist communities if they wanted to. Parts of the Carrville section even put garages on lanes in the back of houses, so that the street fronts could be more attractive for walking and play. Street layouts throughout took into account the width necessary to run buses on future routes, as well as lining up traffic patterns so that buses could eventually travel easily from one section to another. Areas were zoned so that corner stores would be possible, while the major crossroads were planned for neighborhood shopping areas. Densities would run to around 50 residences

Land for parks and schools has been reserved in Vellore Park, Vaughn, Ontario, but no concrete plans for their development have been made yet.

per hectare (about 20 per acre), which works out to about a 170 people per hectare (just under 70 per acre). It looked, on paper at least, like the new developments would be part of a trend toward slowing urban sprawl and be more interesting, environmentally- friendly places to live.

But does this mean much when it comes to real changes in the way people live? Certainly a visit to the internet bulletin board of Cornell, supposedly the purest New Urbanist community around Toronto, suggests that two purported advantages of the New Urbanism, more compact neighborhoods and more emphasis on walking, haven't materialized. As one young, enthusiastic home-buyer wrote in the spring of 2007, "We've driven around the neighborhood a few times but cannot seem to locate any plazas nearby. Where's the nearest Tim Horton's? Where do you get your groceries? Closest movie theatre? … Cornell was supposed to be a pedestrian-friendly area so I was hoping to find all these within walking distance." People who lived there replied that outside a limited area of the original development where housing and office space went up together, there aren't many shops that residents can walk to.

If that is the situation in Cornell, a New Urbanism poster community, what is it like elsewhere? As we start off down Vellore Park Avenue in Vaughan, it quickly becomes clear that it's worse.

The houses on this curving street were finished in the summer of 2007, early enough in the season for some people to enjoy gardens and grass. Over a block and down two streets is a corner lot where someone has devoted much time and love to putting in tomatoes, runner beans, flowers, squash. It is a garden with enough produce to feed a family, a garden that might be a dream fulfilled for someone who never before had enough space. But no one else on the street appears to have lavished as much attention on the yard, although they have neatly trimmed lawns and most boast some end-of-season fall flowers—stalwart rudbeckia, begonias still in bloom, a well-tended rosebush with two last yellow flowers. Halloween is still three weeks away, but already three houses have decorations at their doors—a scarecrow, pumpkin cut-outs, brooms and hay bales. The neat greenness of the front yards in this block contrasts sharply with space directly across the street, which appears to be where the earth was moved when the lots were leveled. A few weeds grow there, along with signs that say the space may eventually be used for one or more schools.

There are no trees, but that's not surprising. E. P. Taylor was the exception, not the rule, among developers when he insisted that trees already growing on the Don Mills site be preserved. In Vellore Park it's unlikely that many trees graced the landscape anyway, since this was farmland, cleared a century or more ago. At the northern edge of the development a ravine cuts diagonally across it; plans call for the water-course and the stream that formed it to be incorporated into a region-wide ecological reserve. There will be trails and protected wet-lands, but at the moment that plan is unrealized.

Here the streets are paved, and streetlights in place. It rained yesterday, but we can walk without getting muddy. We have to walk in the street, though, because one of the tradeoffs in this particular section was an exchange for more space in front of garages instead of sidewalks. Each house has a double garage, in front, but apparently the developers thought that the setback from the street would not be sufficient to park extra cars in the driveway without infringing on a sidewalk. Better no sidewalks at all than having cars protrude on them.

Vellore Park purports to incorporate New Urbanist principles into suburban development, but initially, at least, automobiles are essential and pedestrians must walk on the street.

At this point in the middle of the afternoon, few children are out playing, but we pass two young women pushing strollers, apparently going to visit friends. There are no other adults on foot. We switch over so that we're walking facing traffic, as if we were on a country road, although looking at the houses on their 7.6- to 9-meter (25- or 30-foot-wide) lots it's very clear that this is not country.

The houses in this section are either detached, with a small space between each, or semi-detached, with a common wall on one side. Lots are no bigger than those found in center-city residential areas. The yards are not very deep in back, but fifty years from now, given some careful tree-planting, that side of the street could look as pleasantly compact as Jane Jacobs' street in the Annex. Many of the architectural details are the same, too—porches, gables, brick. Obviously the builders like the look of early twentieth-century semi-suburban neighborhoods. As for the side of the street we're walking down, it could end up as a park or a schoolyard, but while the land is zoned for public use, the decisions on just what that might be are in the future.

A difference between Vellore Park and the Annex, which is unlikely to change, is the distance one has to go to run the simplest errand. Had we started off from Jane Jacobs' house, we'd be shopping on Bloor Street in the time it takes us to make it only halfway past the empty lot. Even when Jacobs' house on Albany was new, in the 1920s, Bloor bustled with activity, and a streetcar ran regularly; there was a small store nearby where children could be sent safely on errands, and from which carrying home a few groceries would not be a chore. But the little map our friends have drawn for us suggests that we haven't even gone a quarter of the way to the nearest place to buy anything. In some respects this sort of development produces many of the disadvantages of living in a tightly-packed inner city residential area, like noise from neighbors and back windows which look out on other back windows, without the advantages of having shops a short walk away and jobs that one can get to by public transit, bike or foot.

The application of New Urbanist ideas have produced higher densities in Cornell in nearby Markham; one recent study shows that the mean gross residential density there is more than 75 percent higher than in Markham's conventional suburban areas. Another study shows that nearly half of Cornell's housing units (42.7 percent) are row- and townhouses. That is much higher than either the rest of Markham or Toronto's inner-city residential neighborhoods, which both run about 10 percent. But the latter study of more than two hundred randomly selected households also showed that more than 80 percent of respondents would choose a single-family, detached house if they could next time. (The study showed housing prices in Cornell comparable to those for similarly-sized dwellings elsewhere in Toronto, leading the author Andrejs Skaburskis to comment, "Unlike some of the early new urbanist communities, Cornell is not an 'elitist' enclave.")

We turn off Vellore Park Avenue at Canada Drive. Houses are under construction here, with people and equipment hard at work preparing homes for more new families. The wind picks up, blowing some grit around. We are about halfway to the nearest store.

Bus service is supposed to be extended to the development in 2008, but there is no word on just what that will consist of. Cityview Boulevard, which runs up Vellore Park's east side, was specifically laid out with buses in mind. Not only is it wide enough for buses to pass, the curves and corners are engineered so that buses can easily handle them. At a future date, multiple units of some sort will go in along Cityview, providing a kind of buffer between the residential area and a major expressway, Highway 400, a little farther east. Currently a rush-hour bus connects with some light industrial and commercial buildings near the Highway 400 overpass, but to get to it from Vellore Park we'd have to hike over muddy fields and, we think, scale a chain-link fence. As was the case in Don Mills, the people who work on the fringes of Vellore Park aren't expected to be able to afford to live here. The only other nearby bus line runs up Weston Road as far as Major Mackenzie Road, one of the region's major thoroughfares, but no farther.

The next bus on Weston will leave from the intersection a little before 3 p.m., headed south. We're not going to take a bus, but we turn left off Canada Drive and walk south on Weston. This is one of the major north-south roads in the area, which once upon a time led north along straight-as-a-die concession lines. Across the road we can see fields; this was an area of market gardens and farms. Italian immigrants settled here and farmed the fertile land, which became the pride of Toronto's agriculture. So persuasive is this group's influence that the final "e" in Vellore is frequently pronounced, making the name sound like a variant of the Italian word for flying, "volare." But in fact the name is Indian, chosen in 1854 when residents of the small village then consisting of a few buildings and a school (established in 1837) applied to get a post office. The British had recently been victorious at Vellore in what is now Tamil Nadu, and the patriotic residents decided to commemorate the triumph.

We have to walk on the road here, too, because sidewalks have yet to be put in. There is more traffic than on the streets inside the development, but this afternoon no one is racing down Weston. Some nights that's not true. The Woodbridge section of Vaughan, just south of Major Mackenzie, is notorious for street racing, prompting documentary films and YouTube videos about young men and their souped-up cars. (For an example, see "Woodbridge Street Racing" in Notes to Chapter 8). Street racing on the back roads has become such a problem, in fact, that in September 2007, new bylaws mandated $2,000 fines and a week's impoundment of the speeder's car for anyone caught doing more than 50 kilometers (about 30 miles) an hour over the speed limit. And it's not just the young and reckless in this part of suburbia who get caught up in the glamor of cars and racing; in January 2008, an 85-year-old was stopped after being clocked at 161 kilometers (nearly 100 miles) an hour on nearby Highway 407, where the legal speed limit is 100 kilometers (60 miles) per hour.

The wind is picking up, but ahead there are some buildings which look like they might house a convenience store. Encouraged, we move along a little faster, taking care to stay to the side of the road. Before we get there, we see that while a drive-in milk and snack store might once have been here, it has been closed for some time: windows are covered up and there's a "Closed" sign on the door.

So we trudge onward, past what looks like a machine shed for farm equipment toward Major Mackenzie Road. From a distance we can see asphalt and concrete driveways suggesting that there is a mini-mall here where we'll have no trouble finding what we want. But hey, look up there on the left. Before we get to the intersection, there's a building which looks like it's been around for decades and seems to be still in operation. There are Halloween decorations in front, including what appears to be a giant pumpkin. As we turn into the driveway, we pass what must have been the counters where fresh farm produce was displayed not so long ago when this area was rural. Inside the little store there are more pumpkins and cornstalks to put beside the door for the upcoming holiday. It has milk, too, but the bread looks past its best-before date, so we briefly consider hiking a bit farther to shop in the little mall across the way. But we've walked enough and we decide we'll buy four liters of milk and then head back. At the counter there are Halloween candies, and we pick up a couple for the kids. There will no doubt be lots of foot traffic in Vellore Park Halloween night, even if ordinarily it is the car that's king.

A year or so before her death, Jane Jacobs visited Vaughan, looking for examples of new small industries which, defying economic predictions, were springing up in the Greater Toronto Area. She was interested in the tool-and-die making factories, the ones making items for the construction industry, kitchen cabinet manufacturers, and the like. They seemed to be examples of her "import replacing" activity, which she found encouraging. Vaughan, however, didn't impress her. It was just a "thoroughly car-dependent suburb" with the only inviting streetscape to be found well south of Vellore Park where the old village of Woodbridge survives in "a tiny heart of shops around a public square … where one actually sees human beings walking."

In many parts of the urban planning universe Toronto is held up as an example of North America's best urban practices. Local and provincial government have a strong commitment to public transportation and greenbelt planning. The provincial "Places to Grow Act," passed in 2005, protects a great arc of farmland and forest surrounding the city as well as several other large municipalities including Hamilton, once Canada's Steeltown. The central districts of Toronto itself, in part because of the influence of Jane Jacobs and her friends, were protected from wholesale destruction in the 1960s and 1970s. In many parts of the city, you don't have to drive. In some respects it is, like Portland, Oregon, an urban planners' dream.

Once you move out to the edges, though, you can't get along without a car except perhaps in rather exotic, inward-looking places like Peace Village, on the other side of Highway 400 from Vellore Park. Built around a large and imposing mosque with rush-hour bus service to and from the nearest subway station, it prides itself on its walkability. "After the children come home from school, they go to the playgrounds close to the Mosque, and at the prayer times they all rush to the Mosque," the group's website boasts. "Our seniors, who previously were getting bored staying at home all the time, now have friends living at walking distances from their homes. They are not dependent on their children to drive them to the Mosque. Our ladies now can take their children to the educational classes being regularly held every weekend at the Mosque, without any fear or intimidation."

"How quaint," some might say, just as others would say "how quaint" about Seaside, Duany and Plater-Zyberk's first New Urbanist creation. Seaside is, Witold Rybczynski wrote, "a small town in the same way that a dude ranch is a ranch, or a bed-and-breakfast is a home that just happens to have guest rooms." In other words, there is a huge difference between walkable neighborhoods that work for many ordinary people from different backgrounds, and those developed for a particular clientèle.

What does this mean for the future of our cities, and for our health?

CHAPTER 9

El Camino Real, Carlsbad, California
The Mall as Substitute

BETTY YORK HAD NOT BEEN much of a walker since she had been a student at UCLA decades ago and now her doctor was giving her an ultimatum: get some exercise or else! She was recovering from a double coronary bypass, and exercise would be essential to her recovery.

" 'Walk,' he said, and I just looked at him. You know, where I live, it's all up hill and down dale. Where could I walk? There aren't any sidewalks either, and I'm not all that spry. So I told him it was out of the question."

A solidly-built woman but not overweight, she had thickened through her middle, over her shoulders, in her bust as the years passed. "He just said, 'Twenty minutes a day, three days a week at the mall or once a week for an hour,' and that's when I became a mall walker."

She laughed. Her curly, once-jet-black hair was now frosted with white, and the flesh under her chin wiggled a bit, but she never went out without elaborate earrings and carefully-applied lipstick and eye makeup. "Mall walker," she said, giving her shoulders a little shake that bordered on the seductive. "Not streetwalker. There's a world of difference, you know."

By the two-thirds mark of the twentieth century, most North American cities had become devoid of streets which invited walking. Nearly everyone drove to work and going on foot to a corner store for a couple of forgotten staples or to pickup Chinese take-out or pizza at a neighborhood restaurant was impossible. Commercial areas were too far away from residential areas. Along stretches of streets on the fringes of many cities, walking was considered out and out dangerous because of the traffic, while in more central districts fear of attack frightened many out of walking. The result was that the habit of going on foot anywhere disappeared from daily life. The consequences of this big change in the way people live were not apparent immediately. Rather than be concerned about this, many, perhaps most, North Americans were delighted to move to new, more spacious, greener, easier communities where they could drive practically everywhere. But not walking has profound effects on our health because, as we saw when we took a look at the way we evolved on the East African savannah, not only might our boots be made for walking, our bodies are too.

Ironically, the current increase in the number of people judged overweight is also due to mechanisms that served us well on the savannah. We like sweet and fat and salty tastes because the natural foods that provide them were not that plentiful when we were hunters and gatherers. People who sought out sweet fruit, sucked the fat from bone marrow, and relished the salty taste of blood, or their equivalents, were likely to be better nourished than those who didn't. These healthier folk subsequently left more offspring behind. We may be a little like pythons who swallow rodents whole when they get a chance, and then are able to survive long periods without eating. As J. Eric Oliver says in his careful study of the obesity situation, *Fat Politics: The Real Story Behind America's Obesity Epidemic*, fatness is "a protective mechanism that evolved to survive fluctuations in our food supply … In conditions of privation, our extra weight may be exactly what we need to survive. … The problem arises from the interaction between these adaptive mechanisms and our current environment. In other words … we are in a situation for which we are ill-adapted."

How this imbalance between food and exercise shows up can be seen all around the world. Take for example the high rates of diabetes among Amerindians and Inuit no longer relying on their traditional way of life for food. Having successfully adapted to cycles of feast and famine, their genetic heritage makes them tragically susceptible to the downside of excess. On the other hand, Cubans, forced to walk more and eat less in the difficult decade after the USSR collapsed and support from the Soviet Union disappeared, actually appear to be healthier: mortality from diabetes has fallen, as did the incidence of cardiovascular disease.

"So what if our lifestyles makes us fat?" the skeptic might ask. There have always been obese people. Think of Henry VIII in the dashing portrait by Holbein, or those corpulent nudes that Renoir doted on, not to mention Mrs. Mingott, the doyenne of mid-nineteenth century New York society in Martin Scorsese's version of Edith Wharton's *The Age of Innocence*. She could no longer go up and down stairs since "flesh had descended on her" and so had transformed one of her sitting rooms into a bedroom. The "foreignness of this arrangement recalled scenes in French fiction," the voice-over narrative tells us.

These cases, please note, are exceptions. The ordinary run of mortals, until very recently, were not fat. To have leisure and more than enough to eat meant one was very well off. Thus corpulence denoted high status.

It doesn't today. Take a look at the buff bodies of celebrities in any photo magazine, or remember the fun poked at George W. Bush's plumper daughter Jenna shortly after her engagement was announced, and the ridicule Sarah Ferguson provoked when she ballooned up after her marriage to Prince Andrew broke up. Chubby is definitely down-market these days, in part because it is so common.

How did this happen? People are eating more than they used to. Oliver quotes figures from the U.S. Centers for Disease Control showing American women consuming 335 more calories daily in the early twenty-first century than they did in the 1970s, while men consumed 168 more. The U.S. Department of Agriculture has a different breakdown—268 more calories for men and 143 for women—but the effect is the same. It doesn't sound like much, but it adds up. One study with anorexics suggests that about 10,000 excess calories are required to gain a kilogram of weight, which means that if a woman eats 335 excess calories daily, she'll gain a kilo (2.2 pounds) in about a month. Do that for five years, and she could find herself more than 60 kilograms (132 pounds) over her starting weight. If you eat more, you gain weight, all things being equal.

And things are not equal. North Americans appear to be eating more, and in most places they are spending more time in cars than they did thirty years ago. A telling example comes from the statistics on how kids get to school. It used to be—only a generation ago in fact—that more than 40 percent of American children rode bikes or walked to school. Safer streets and better schools are top reasons why people say they move to the suburbs, and classic suburban development planned an elementary school at the center of each new neighborhood. In the early twenty-first century, though, various studies show that the proportion of kids getting to school on their own power has radicallly declined: now more than 80 per cent of American kids go in school buses or private cars. Part of this may be due to busing schemes that attempt to balance schools racially, or because of fear of child molesters even in "nice" neighborhoods, but new housing developments are also often more spread out than older ones were, making the distances to travel farther.

It's no surprise that an interesting correlation between urban sprawl and obesity has begun to show up. A study of two hundred thousand people in various parts of the U.S. showed significant differences in the average weights of those who live in the least sprawling and the most sprawling counties studied. Manhattan was the least sprawling, while Geauga County, near Cleveland, Ohio was the most. The difference in weight was 6.3 pounds: the average 5'7" Manhattanite weighed in at 161.1 pounds but the average person from Geauga weighed 167.4 pounds. This was not a back-of-the-envelope calculation, but one using data from an annual survey of the Center for Disease Control's Behavioral Risk Factor Surveillance System. Age, gender, education (as a proxy for income), race or ethnicity, fruit and vegetable consumption and smoking were taken into account. Sprawl was determined by analysis of multiple factors, and the authors are careful to point out the study's shortcomings such as the difficulty of teasing out the other factors that might be involved. Perhaps not surprisingly, the study also found that people who lived in the least sprawling counties were far more likely to walk to work as well as to walk more for leisure.

Other research suggests that the people who choose to live in sprawling neighborhoods may be different from those who don't. It may be that difference, not neighborhood design, which accounts for the fact that obesity is more prevalent in sprawling neighborhoods. Compare the results of a large, well-constructed telephone survey done in 2003 of representative Americans living in many places with a more recent survey of Long Island residents who have chosen a suburban life-style. The first survey showed that 80 percent of Americans would like to walk more, and 54 percent would like to walk "a lot more." The questions asked in the Long Island survey were somewhat different, but it's clear the Long Islanders were much less warm to the idea of walking than the public at large; more than half said they would rather live in a neighborhood where they had to drive, rather than one where they could walk.

The choices people make about how they live also are readily apparent in Mireille Guiliano's best-selling *French Women Don't Get Fat.* "Walking is an essential part of the French way of life, and the average French woman walks three times as much as the average American," she writes. The French are not so eager to take shortcuts when they walk either: "We believe the journey is the destination." She adds that she and her husband always lose weight when they visit Paris, because in that city they walk even more than they do in Manhattan where they live now.

But why should anyone really care what other people weigh? Isn't that a personal choice?

To some extent, yes. But the health effects of extra weight are felt by society as a whole. Possible problems like increased risk of diabetes, heart troubles, and wear and tear on joints mean more pressure on the healthcare system. The extra weight also translates into more petroleum products used. As noted earlier, Americans are now pumping 938 million more gallons of gasoline and diesel annually than in 1960, purely as a result of extra weight in vehicles, over and above extra fuel required to navigate the increasing sprawl. Air pollution from that excess fuel consumption is everybody's business. So are the increased greenhouse gas emissions produced in a sprawling, car-centered world. The most recent Canadian statistics suggest that six thousand deaths a year, 70 percent of them from cardiovascular "events," are caused by air pollution from car and factory exhaust. A larger study in the U.S. reported in 2007 that air pollution can increase the risk of heart disease by 75 percent or more.

Air pollution can be fought in many fashions, including being tougher on tailpipe emissions, but more long-lasting positive effects are accomplished by attacking the problem at its source, and cutting down on the need for automobile use. Improvements from lowering per vehicle pollution can be wiped out if the number of cars on the road increases, just as car engine efficiency gains after the Oil Crisis of the 1970s have since been translated into more power per car, not significantly better mileage.

As Reid Ewing, principle author of the study linking sprawl and obesity says, "The United States needs to redesign its communities to promote physical activity as part of people's daily routines, for example, walking to lunch, climbing stairs, and using transit which requires a walk at each end. This will require higher densities, finer mixes of residential and non-residential activities, stronger downtowns and other activity centers, and smaller blocks for better street accessibility."

But what do we do in the meantime?

What Betty York did was find a nearby mall where she could get some exercise. For most of her married life she had lived in various suburbs of Los Angeles, all upscale and designed with cars, not pedestrians, in mind. So when her doctor commanded walking, her first instinct was to go looking for a classy shopping mall.

She had several within a half-hour drive to choose from, but Plaza Camino Real Mall in Carlsbad was her pick. Its name is redolent of history—walking history. Between 1683 and 1834 Franciscan friars established a series of missions in what is now California and the Mexican state of Baja California. When completed, the chain stretched more than 600 miles (960 kilometers), with missions about 30 miles (48 kilometers) apart, or the distance that a man could walk in a ten- or eleven-hour day. Never more than a track on which a wagon could travel, the road that connected them was known as El Camino Real, the King's Highway. Like the roads the Romans built in France fifteen hundred years before, it generally kept to plateau land where possible. The missions themselves were built near streams or rivers, but high enough above the watercourse to avoid flooding in the sometimes torrential rains of winter.

The mission nearest Betty's favorite shopping mall lay over a ridge of high land in the next watershed to the north. The California coast in this stretch is marked by canyons running roughly east to west and cut by streams that are now frequently covered over or channeled between concrete banks: Buena Vista Creek emerges a bit to the west of Betty's mall to form Buena Vista Lagoon which opens onto the Pacific. Mission San Luis Rey de Francia sits on relatively flat land above the San Luis Rey River; an aqueduct supplied the mission with ample river water from a point upstream. Established in 1798 just as the French Revolution was drawing to its end, the mission was named, probably not coincidently, after Louis IX, the canonized crusader king of France. Surrounded by cultivated fields and cattle, the mission became the largest in Alta California with a population of about twenty-seven hundred before the missions were secularized in 1834. Today its main buildings have been restored and its laundry and gardens excavated so that one can walk in the steps of the missionaries to get an idea of what this country was like two centuries ago.

The Plaza Camino Real mall was built 170 years after the mission was founded, and has been extensively remodeled twice since it opened in the 1960s. Its two levels are home to a nice sprinkling of stores like Abercrombie & Fitch along with less tony shops. Mall walkers are welcome before regular business hours, one morning a week. While Betty York had never heard of the practice, the idea did not origin-ate here, but goes back to one of the first enclosed malls which opened in 1956 in Edina, outside Minneapolis, Minnesota.

The Edina mall was built at the same time as Toronto's Don Mills suburb was nearing completion. This was the time of the great mid-century move out of the city with shopping malls being built to serve the new communities. The saga of the rise of the mall is the story of the end of downtown, with the demise of the neighborhood shopping street as a subplot.

From the beginning of settlement, every town in North America with the slightest pretension claimed a downtown. That was where the court house, law offices, banks, and retail stores were located. Churches were built on the main street or not far off it, while doctors, dentists, and barbershops would be nearby also. While "going to town" was a big event for people from the country, and trips downtown were an impor-tant part of civic life for town dwellers, people who knew bigger, older cities often found small towns provincial. Take the reaction of Carol Kennicott, Sinclair Lewis's heroine in his novel *Main Street*, to her first amble through the downtown of the small city to which her new husband had brought her. What she saw was "not only the heart of a place called Gopher Prairie, but ten thousand towns from Albany to San Diego."

Dyer's Drug Store, a corner building of regular and unreal blocks of artificial stone. ... A small wooden motion-picture theater called "The Rosebud Movie Palace." Lithographs announcing a film called "Fatty in Love." Howland & Gould's Grocery. In the display window, black, overripe bananas and lettuce on which a cat was sleeping ... Dahl & Oleson's Meat Market—a reek of blood ... A jewelry shop with tinny-looking wrist-watches for women. In front of it, at the curb, a huge wooden clock which did not go ... A fly-buzzing saloon with a brilliant gold and enamel whisky sign across the front. Other saloons down the block ... In front of the saloons, farm wives sitting on the seats of wagons, waiting for their husbands to become drunk and ready to start home ... A tobacco shop called "The Smoke House." ... A clothing store with a display of "ox-blood-shade Oxfords with bull-dog toes."

and so on. But chief among them was:

The Bon Ton Store—Haydock & Simons'—the largest shop in town. The first-story front of clear glass, the plates cleverly bound at the edges with brass. The second story of pleasant tapestry brick. One window of excellent clothes for men, interspersed with collars of floral pique which showed mauve daisies on a saffron ground. Newness and an obvious notion of neatness and service. Haydock & Simons. Haydock ... His shop was clean!

A department store with a French name! It was a link with a wider world, a place where some of the excitement of big cities was on display. Just who invented the idea of showcasing many sorts of merchandise in one elegant building, and the accompanying practice of setting non-negotiable prices that allowed shoppers and salespeople to pretend money wasn't important by eliminating haggling, is a topic that raises the ire of those who take their shopping history seriously. As with so many things having to do with taste in the nineteenth century, the French generally get the credit: the Parisian pioneer Au Bon Marché adopted the formula in 1852, just at the beginning of the massive transformation of the city. In his novel *Au Bonheur des dames* (*The Ladies' Delight*), Émile Zola tells the story of its beginning from the point of view of a plucky young woman from the provinces who is captivated by the bustle and exuberance of the new way of selling things. She defends the high-volume, quick-turnover approach to her uncle who is forced out of business by the department store. "You probably are more competent than me," she says at one point, betraying a modesty that Zola seemed to admire, "but I'll say what I'm thinking … Prices, rather than be set as they were before, by fifty businesses, are set today by four or five, and they're lower, thanks to the power of the capital and the strength of their clientèle. It's so much better for the public, that's all."

Reading that is like hearing an apologist for Wal-Mart (although it should be noted that Zola says Au Bon Marché provided healthcare for its staff while Wal-Mart had to be pressured into doing that more than a century later), which perhaps shows again that there's nothing new under the sun. At any rate, the Philadelphia merchant John Wanamaker adapted—or maybe reinvented—the form in the 1870s in his hometown. His success inspired much imitation. By the late nineteenth century all the big cities in the U.S. and Canada had one or more department stores that were not just places for buying but privileged destinations inter-twined with the social life of the city, where women in particular "simply and necessarily went, the way people had once wandered into and out of church," says Adam Gopnik in his essay on New York in *Through the Children's Gate: A Home in New York.*

The form these stores took varied but they were usually built with great attention to detail that signaled to the shopper, you are part of something much bigger and more sophisticated than you will find in other places. The cachet of the French model was translated around the world. In particular the beautiful Art Deco Galéries Lafayette building, opened in Paris in 1912, inspired many imitations. The ten-story building—just flirting with Parisian height limitations—had two large central halls under steel and stained glass domes of which one remains today. Balconies on the different levels circled this open space so that the interior of the store was illuminated from the top down and the eye leapt upwards as in a cathedral. The Marshal Field store in Chicago, whose central space was recently restored, can be seen as an homage to the Parisian landmark, as is La Maison de la Bonneterie in The Hague, Netherlands, which is as charming as it was when it was built in 1913. But the balconies and beautiful light of the aptly named City of Paris

The gorgeous Art Deco interior of the Galéries Lafayette in Paris served as a model for department stores around the world.

Suburban shopping malls, like Montreal's Rockland Center, gave downtown shopping districts great competition.

department store in San Francisco disappeared under the wreckers' ball in the 1970s.

By then department stores in downtowns all over North America were finding times tough. Malls were taking more and more business as city centers in the U.S., although less so in Canada, emptied out. The ideal mall had two department stores, one on each end. Each catered to a slightly different market, like Sears and Lord and Taylor perhaps. According to Richard S. Tedlow, a professor at the Harvard Business School who has written extensively on the subject, the shops that filled the mall between the two anchors got a free ride. They didn't have to advertise to attract shoppers, since they could rely on the attraction of the big stores to generate foot traffic.

In this way they were rather like the small stores that have always lined a healthy shopping street. The fact that the shops were clustered together meant that shoppers, who might not go out of their way to visit them, would be tempted to enter on their way somewhere else. Tedlow says that over time the small retailers became more skilled at marketing a limited range of goods, leaving the department stores struggling to be everything to everyone. The big stores suffered, frequently trying to reinvent themselves as collections of boutiques. Competition further increased when discount retailers like Wal-Mart and Costco set up big-box stores at locations often near, but usually not in, shopping malls. These new retail outlets charged lower prices; their profit came from greater volume and because the massive orders they placed allowed them to wring lower wholesale prices from suppliers.

To attract foot traffic and encourage people to make the mall part of their life, malls invite groups of people, usually elderly or on the verge of retirement, to get their exercise walking the malls' interior streets. They may not be big spenders, but they are likely to buy coffee and goodies on a regular basis, and to feel kindly toward the mall, returning again when they have larger purchases to make.

A distinction should be made between this kind of mall with upwards of fifty stores and acres of parking and the little strip mall which became the suburban equivalent of a shopping street. In its classic form the strip mall has anywhere from six to twenty or so storefronts facing on a parking lot. A grocery store might serve as a sort of anchor, but not necessarily. This is not a "destination" mall, that is, a mall where people go to be entertained or to do serious shopping. Strip malls are places to drive to for milk and magazines, to pick up some Thai take-out, or retrieve clothes from the cleaners. Frequently they were constructed when a particular residential area was first laid out, and were intended to serve the immediately surrounding area. But the marketing assumptions made then often were wrong: the strip mall might be poorly located, or too close to another, or undercut by the arrival of a nearby super grocery and drugstore complex. Malls of this size with boarded-up store fronts and weeds breaking up the pavement in parking lots are a common site. One estimate puts the number of "dead" malls in the U.S. at fifteen hundred, while shopping-mall guru Paco Underhill jokes that the string of empty strip malls would stretch to the moon, if set side by side.

There was a small strip mall not far from Betty York's home. Its video store was where she picked up a movie a couple of nights a week, and the veterinarian who had her offices there looked after Betty's cat. But Betty would not think of walking that mall for exercise, in part because it is open to the elements, but also because she might run into one of her neighbors.

"I never wore running shoes before, I never wore anything like them except when I played tennis fifty years ago when I was a girl," she said as she got out of her car and prepared to meet her mall-walking friends. "But the woman who organizes this said that a good pair of shoes would make all the difference in the world." She smiled. She still had high-heeled sandals on. She didn't want to change into sensible shoes until the last minute.

At the door a handful of other walkers were already waiting for the mall to open. On the other side the guard grinned, teasing them as he counted down the seconds until 8:30 a.m. on his fingers. Then he opened the doors, and the crowd, suddenly larger, with a half dozen new arrivals, surged inside.

Betty had her running shoes in her tote bag and she went over to sit down on one of the benches that circle the fountain in the middle of the mall space. As she slipped off her handsome sandals, and pulled on her socks, she talked with the other women also suiting up for their workout. Later she said that she met people who live on the same hillside as she does, but whom she'd never seen before. Her retirement complex

Small strip malls were designed to provide everyday services to suburban communities, but many have struggled against competition from larger, newer shopping centers. Unlike the shopping streets of walkable neighborhoods they usually get little foot traffic.

has a bridge club and a pool, but somehow they'd never crossed paths.

Crossed paths: it's a metaphor grounded in the reality of another time. Neither Betty nor her friends seemed to see any irony in it. Their attention turned to the young woman hired to ride herd on the mall walkers. She greeted them all and then opened the empty store front where they would start out with a few warm-up exercises.

About that empty store: there was more than one on this level of the mall, and even though the mall's major tenants seemed to be doing well, it was rumored to be heading for a major makeover. Jane Jacobs talked frequently about the human desire for novelty, for liveliness and new challenges. For her, a main advantage of a neighborhood where people walked was the chance to see new things, and the opportunity that buildings of differing ages gave to entrepreneurs who want to make and sell new products and ideas. If one keeps that in mind, it should be no surprise that malls lose their attraction after a while, particularly if the owners allow maintenance to slide a bit and if the demographics of the particular region change.

One of the features of an automobile-based society is that it gives legs to this fickleness. How far a shopper has to drive may affect the decision of where to shop somewhat, but once he or she is in a car, whether the distance is five kilometers or fifteen is usually immaterial, as long as there is plenty of parking, and provided that highway access is relatively easy. Not having nearby public transportation can be considered a plus since the people who use it—often car-less teenagers and minority group members—may not be the clientèle the mall wants to attract, Underhill says in his engaging book *The Call of the Mall*. He recounts how the family of one young African-American woman killed crossing a busy thoroughfare because buses were not allowed to stop at a mall, successfully sued it, arguing that the prohibition was based on racial discrimination.

Nevertheless, other malls cater to the teenage market with video arcades and movie theaters, bowling alleys and miniature golf in an effort to distinguish themselves from the competition. But these are, it appears, controlled imitations of what might happen in the old city. Underhill quotes one teenage girl describing what her perfect mall might include: "I don't know if you've ever been to Washington Square in New York," she began, "but it's this park, and they have these tables with, like, built-in checkerboards on top?"

To make malls livelier, they often include kiosks that display a variety of products that might not sell enough to warrant paying rent for a whole store. Betty's mall was featuring a magician and his wares on the second level during the winter of 2007-2008. Underhill compares the operators of these kiosks to the merchants on old shopping streets because they have to know much more about their market and their products than the store managers of the chain stores in the mall. "I don't mean to pick on them—it's not their fault that their employers expect so little of them," he writes. "That's the nature of large, centralized corporations today, where all the meaningful decisions are made in a single office, by men and women who spend as little time as possible on the selling floor."

This disconnect as well as the desire for something new has led to a recent development: the "lifestyle center" where shops and stores are set on a "main street" in imitation of an old-fashioned Main Street. The center features an open area of shops and stores facing each other across a street open to the elements that is supposed to resemble a small town shopping street. Offices and housing units are sometimes located on the second floors of the buildings, and the vertical scale usually is low. The first of these centers was opened in 1986 in Tennessee, with the stated purpose of providing a "unique shopping experience" with an "organic feel." Since then they have stolen the thunder from other sorts of shopping centers. While big enclosed malls continued to be built for another twenty years after the first lifestyle center—eight opened in the U.S. between 2003 and 2006—no new ones are planned at the moment in the U.S. By 2007, there were nearly two hundred "topless" malls, according to the International Council of Shopping Centers. Compare that with eleven hundred enclosed malls and countless small strip malls, and it's clear that this new kind of selling still has a relatively small share of the market. But it's all that city officials and developers are talking about as the former push for new construction and the latter chase the consumer's dollar.

Betty York's mall in Carlsbad and one in Escondido, about 45 miles (about 70 kilometers) inland, were bought recently by the Australian property development company Westfield. The owner of fifty-nine malls in the U.S. and sixty-one elsewhere in the world including twelve in Canada (the former TrizecHahn group), Westfield has upgraded several malls by adding outdoor components which take a page from the lifestyle center book. Movers and shakers in Carlsbad and Escondido would like to see both their malls catch the wave. Escon-dido's city council stirred much discussion in the fall of 2007 when it considered zoning changes that would allow Westfield North County mall to retool and grow. Currently it has Nordstrom, Macy's, Sears, and J. C. Penney as anchor department stores, plus 182 specialty stores, 5,702 parking spaces and a food court with twelve restaurants. But a series of stories about the proposal in the *North County News* prompted some harsh attacks on the kind of people who frequent the mall. The subtext in the comments on the newspaper's website was that the demographics of the area had changed—a much larger Latino population lives there than twenty years ago—and some parts of the white middle class don't like that.

This ethnic and economic shift in suburban population reflects the fact that millions of North Americans, no matter what their race or ethnic origin, dream of a house set in its own garden. Finding that kind of housing has usually meant looking on the suburban outskirts of cities, but rising prices in the early twenty-first century sent people looking farther and farther into countryside. What this means for Betty's mall is that its clientèle is likely to change and that as malls jockey to maintain and increase their market shares, competition will be rough. The small city of San Marcos, which is the next municipality inland from where Betty lived, has recently begun a zoning and development plan which is designed to provide more lifestyle center shopping and housing in a downtown that really is a downtown. Escondido also would like to gussie up its old downtown—as would a thousand other municipalities across North America. Indeed, the number of "lifestyle downtown" plans in the works makes one think of the great movement toward pedestrian malls in downtowns during the 1970s. The projects included making Sparks Street in downtown Ottawa, a no-car mall, re doing downtown Hamilton so it would look like a shopping center, and removing cars from the center of Fresno, California. Pressure to undertake the frequently very costly projects came from merchants and property owners who were terrified by the competition coming from the burgeoning number of suburban shopping centers. Not many of them were successful, which should make developers and planners wonder what they have to do this time to do it right.

But Betty York won't see if Westfield Plaza Camino Real will be surrounded by four hundred new apartments and "courtyard homes" with 400,000 square feet (about 40,000 square meters) of commercial space added and some new freestanding stores grouped around an ersatz main street, as Carlsbad planners would like. Betty died a few years ago in her eighties, having lived much longer than she thought she would when her heart problems began. Like those Cubans who grew healthier when they had to walk, she may have profited greatly from her regular mall workouts. Certainly mall walking got her out of the house and out of the car for years.

Time now for us to climb in the car and drive off into the traffic that is becoming ever heavier in the growing Southern California conurbation. Look there, though, at that poster for a community activity Plaza Camino Real has become involved in. It says that the mall is now an official sponsor of the campaign against childhood obesity. The promotional material proclaims: "Westfield is giving a gift that will keep on giving for the rest of their lives—a healthy lifestyle." The property development company says it is working with First 5 California, a California organization "dedicated to the health and well being of children ages five and younger," to promote "healthier choices for young children." The current campaign advises "offering healthy snacks ... such as carrots and fruit," and only allowing a certain amount of sweet things a day.

A laudable effort, certainly. Too bad, though, that there isn't also a mention of getting the kids out walking.

The percentage of North American children walking to school has been declining for thirty years, a fact which many experts think contributes to childhood obesity.

CHAPTER 10

Keith Road, North Vancouver, B.C.
Logging Road to Trail to the Future

THE SUN SETS in summer much later in North Vancouver than it does in Carlsbad because it is so much farther north, but evenings in both places have the same magic glow about them: fine pink light fading into darkness, the smell of salt water not too far away, brilliant flowers. It's a good evening to take the dog out for a walk, and Kris Down says we can join her.

She, her partner Alex and their pug Maxine live on the first floor of what was built as a single-family, detached house in this suburb of Vancouver, British Columbia, which may be pointing the way towards making North American cities more walkable. They don't have the view of mountains and sea that some houses and apartments in the region have, largely because the hillside on which they live is part of the magnificent backdrop that makes Vancouver famous. Not far from their house, their hillside rises to become part of the grand mountain chain which runs along the north shore of the fjords and delta of the Fraser River. Nearby is Grouse Mountain, probably the most startling peak one can reach by regular public transportation in North America. Buses run frequently from Lonsdale Quay at sea level to the ski lift near the top; it's a single bus ticket from downtown Vancouver, including a ride on the SeaBus across Burrard Inlet to the Quay. Grouse Mountain rises 1,177 meters (3,861 feet) above sea level: other peaks surrounding it are similarly impressive. Often the mountaintops are covered with feet of snow late into June when dry, warm summer weather has arrived in North Van.

When the missions in California were being built, the future United States was rebeling against Britain, France was poised before its own

North Vancouver mixes apartments with retail and commercial development in a spectacular waterside setting.

jump into revolution, and Spanish and British explorers were sailing through the nearby waters of what is now called the Georgia Strait that separates the mainland from Vancouver Island. These slopes were covered by cedars and other magnificent trees that were hundreds of years old. The Coast Salish Native Canadian population lived along the shoreline, with the hillsides to their back. While they did some hunting and wild food-gathering on the slopes, they spent more time on the sea than hiking the hillsides. And while they used red cedar logs to make dugout canoes as long as 9 meters (30 feet) and for the ridge beams for houses that were often longer, the stands of timber were essentially untouched. That changed in the mid-nineteenth century when Europeans arrived. Logging operations began in the 1860s, and by the end of the century the easily available big trees had been cut.

Kris lives on the corner of Moody Street, which is named after Sewell Prescott Moody, who made a fortune from those trees. His sawmill operations were down the hill a bit in Moodyville, a community that quickly faded once the mill closed in 1901. Walking out Kris's door now on a summer night, we see no trace of that long-gone forest. Her street, running east and west, is relatively flat, and while trees high up on mountains are visible, it is clear that the trees that are near us have been planted for shade or fruit in the last fifty years or so. We'd see hints of what the forest must have been like were we to take Max on her very favorite walk: it starts a short drive up the mountainside in Lynn Valley Regional Park. The Lynn River comes down from the high country here, and the gently rising walk into the park follows what once was an old logging road. Heavy equipment abandoned a century ago or more lies rusting along the way, while up the hillside the ghosts of big trees lurk in stumps that have not quite yet rotted away despite the passage of time. But where we are going to walk this evening, the terrain has been tamed with grids of streets laid over the old forests.

Like Manhattan, North Vancouver (incorporated as a city in 1907) was originally organized in grids extending back from the waterfront. The coastline is not a straight line, of course. It slides southward and eastward with zigs and zags which meant that the different grids eventually had to be fitted together at oblique angles. Kris lives one street south of Keith Road, the first thoroughfare built across this part of the steep mountainside in 1912. Its construction required slashing through what remained of the forest and filling in swamps. Local histories say that in places the road was washed away more than once in landslides that came when torrential rains soaked the denuded hillside. Now the road, which is called Marine Drive further east and west, jogs several times to reflect the shoreline.

It is early evening when we set out. The sun has started its descent in the sky. In an hour or so it will disappear behind Vancouver Island, directly west from the end of Kris's street, and even now it has begun to cast long shadows. Max races out the door and runs wide, exuberant circles around us. After we cross the lawn we put her on a leash and turn at the corner onto Moody. The street climbs quickly: one of the disadvantages of a grid street layout is that it almost always disregards topography. Kris usually walks down the hill to catch her bus to work in the morning, but the haul up is so steep that she'll go another stop so she can connect with a hill-climbing route when she comes home.

After these hills were logged and Moody's mill closed, settlement in North Vancouver shifted west a bit. In the 1880s several well-heeled investors acquired large tracts of land running back from the waterfront and encompassing most of what is now the city of North Vancouver

Victoria Park was created when North Vancouver was laid out as a traditional suburb at the beginning of the twentieth century, but the city is now becoming denser with infill construction like the apartments on the left.

(the District of North Vancouver surrounds the city to the north and east). The men's names live on in the names of streets, although who they were seems more or less forgotten. Lonsdale, the main north-south street, which is now a major shopping and business axis, seems to commemorate a young British army officer, Henry Heywood-Lonsdale, who was one of the principal shareholders in the property company (James Cooper Keith was another). Born in 1864, Heywood-Lonsdale was back in England by 1897, apparently never to return to British Columbia, but his name survives not only in Lonsdale Avenue but in Heywood Park, one of several that cut through the city along the lines of water courses.

With easily accessible forest more or less exhausted, fishing and ship-building soon became the main industries for the north shore. During World War II North Vancouver shipyards produced 35 per cent of the ships which ferried troops and equipment between Canada and Europe. Although the city plan called for a set of wide green boulevards, during the Depression and World War II housing for workers took priority, with many small houses built on lots 8 meters (about 25 feet) wide within walking distance of the industrial plants. It was not until after 1945 that the hillsides were subdivided and middle-class housing like Kris's was built.

At the corner of Keith and Moody is a small corner store which sells groceries and house plants, an interesting combination in this suburb full of lawns and gardens. We walk along Keith toward Victoria Park. The street is divided here, with a green median. The two arms open wide at the park, embracing the long green space with its cenotaph dating from 1923 and now honoring the dead of the Boer War and both World Wars. At the corner of Lonsdale a watering trough for horses still sits just inside the park; when horsepower was the only way to get up the hills the animals often needed to stop and drink. But Max, whose legs are very short, persuades us to turn back well before we get that far. We head in the other direction in the settling twilight. A bus passes going east. Another one passes going west.

Even though the layout of the neighborhood features rather large lots, the overall density in North Vancouver is high—about 37 dwelling units per hectare (16 units per acre) in this section, a figure to compare with the 9.6 units per hectare (4.9 per acre) that Don Mills boasts in Toronto. Greater density is being encouraged. Just a block north of here, the conversion of a duplex into a triplex received not only the approval of neighbors but the distinction of being named a "best practices" example by the Metro Vancouver planning council.

But this is not the dense part of North Van, nor even near its center. The area along the water, which slowly was converted from industrial uses in the 1970s and '80s, saw much apartment building. When the SeaBus—regular pedestrian ferry service to downtown Vancouver—went into operation in 1977, residential development increased.

Kris moved to North Van with a girlfriend when she was ready to take flight from her parents' home in the tony Keresdale district of Vancouver. The north shore wasn't a first choice, but they couldn't find anything they liked and could afford in the city itself. Besides, the SeaBus made the commute to downtown easy, and so they took a two-bedroom flat within walking distance of the ferry terminal and the Lonsdale Quay which was just beginning to develop as a market and shop complex. When she and Alex hooked up there was no question of moving to any other place; no other district offered as much for a price a young couple could afford.

Max likes the neighborhood a lot. She snuffles up the street, reveling in the smells that make a landscape so fascinating to dogs. There's an elementary school two blocks away, so perhaps she's picking up odors of lost Pop Tarts or discarded sandwiches. Or maybe she's just learning which of the other neighborhood dogs has been out promenading too. Kris has to encourage her to move along as we continue to saunter past neat houses. Sprinklers run, music comes through an open window, the moon begins to float above the mountains. We walk east, past Moody to the next street, Queensbury, where the bus runs which Kris takes up the hill many days. As we turn down the street, the skyline of Vancouver, with its new skyscrapers, and Burrard Inlet, with its ships at dock, lie before us.

It is on this street that the genius of North Van becomes apparent. This is not a suburb where you are completely dependent on your car; it offers the choices that go with interesting urban life. Off to the right we can see the tops of cranes working on the high-rise apartments near the SeaBus terminal. At the corner, a family has invested a lot in garden design, with tall cedar hedging around a corner lot and prize plantings visible inside. But there also are a few businesses: the Queensbury Market, an Italian restaurant, and the Mount Royal Bagel Shop. How long they've been there is not clear, but obviously North Van allows this kind of mixed usage, and the community supports it enough to keep the shops open.

Max knows we're almost home now and trots eagerly down the sidewalk. There's Kris's place on the corner. Alex is out, getting something from the SUV he uses for his work in the building trades. It's nearly dark. The streetlamps are on and a million lights show across the water in downtown Vancouver. The people downstairs—the owners who live in the bottom half of the house which opens out onto a big backyard—drive up. Kris waves. The evening smells of petunias and cut grass and someone barbecuing.

Christopher B. Leinberger didn't look at Canadian cities in his report for the Brookings Institution on walkable cities, *Footloose and Fancy Free: A Field Survey of Walkable Urban Places in the Top 30 U.S. Metropolitan Areas,* released in fall 2007. Had he done so, several Greater Vancouver neighborhoods would have been included in the list of places where density, walkability and transit work together to produce extremely pleasant urban areas which are better designed to respond to the challenges we face. Seattle ranked sixth in Leinberger's most walkable cities line-up, with one walkable neighborhood per half-million people, but Vancouver clearly would rate much better. Take the fact that a typical car or truck in Vancouver was traveling about 24 kilometers (about 15 miles) a day in 1999, while its opposite number in Seattle traveled 19 miles (about 31 kilometers) a day because only a quarter of Seattle's population lived in compact neighborhoods.

Leinberger counts a hundred and fifty-seven walkable places in the U.S. ranging from neighborhoods adjacent to downtowns like Jane Jacobs' Greenwich Village, to developments on the fringes of cities like the Reston Town Center outside Washington, D.C. These walkable areas are found in old downtown areas in the large metropolitan areas or right next to downtown or just a transit stop away from the center city; they are sometimes found in what used to be the downtowns of communities laid out before the rise of the automobile that have been incorporated into the larger city, or in parts of the suburbs which have been redeveloped with higher-density housing and mixed uses, and in new "greenfield" development on the lifestyle-center model. Leinberger cautions that retail-only lifestyle centers shouldn't be included when talking about walkable urban places. You might be able to walk down their imitation main street and saunter into shops, but they don't combine shopping, housing, and work in a walkable environment, so they are, in effect, just another configuration of the shopping mall.

Having said that, it's unclear how he would classify Park Royal Center in West Vancouver, next to North Van, where Kris works at the Whole Foods store. The big grocery, the second one opened in Canada by the food retailer specializing in organic, high quality and locally-sourced products, has pride of place at a section of the center, called The Village. Park Royal Center lies on two sides of a major road, Marine Drive, with a pedestrian and vehicle overpass leading from one side to the other. For a long time Park Royal billed itself as Canada's first enclosed shopping mall, opening as it did in 1950 before the Don Mills Center and about the same time as Seattle's Northgate Mall. Since then it has gone through several re-inventions. The most recent, completed in 2004 at a cost of $30 million CDN, is modeled on the shopping street of a small town, like so many other "lifestyle" shopping complexes. But what sets it apart from many of these new developments is the way it is integrated into the larger mall and the high-rise apartments which are close by. It also is a transportation hub, with buses from other parts of the North Shore and from Vancouver passing through. It is quite possible to live in one of the "view" apartments, commute to downtown Vancouver, and shop, without being dependent on a car.

The mall is much too far to walk from North Vancouver, but it's not a long ride on the bus, which is what Kris often takes. She has to be there early—when you work in the food business a lot of preparation must be done before the shoppers arrive—and traffic isn't too bad. Later on there will be snarls getting onto the Lion's Gate Bridge. The approaches swing around next to Park Royal and frequently traffic headed for downtown Vancouver by way of the bridge and Stanley Park backs up onto Marine Drive. The West Vancouver urban plan calls for encouraging more office space in and around the mall and westward on the other side of the waterfront Ambleside Park. The idea is to provide more work for people on the North Shore: currently 53 percent of West Vancouver residents work outside the municipality, although 17 percent work at home. That's something of a change in West Van's philosophy; it has always taken pains to set itself off from the more working-class neighborhoods to the east, such as North Vancouver, and for a long time it did not encourage commercial or business development. The result was a basically upper-middle-class suburb featuring large houses, many of them with spectacular views and designed to suit the most up-to-date taste. But even here the advantages to more compact development and the problems created when people can't work near where they live have begun to be appreciated.

Jane Jacobs suggests in *Dark Age Ahead* that people who grew up outside North America may take less convincing to opt for more compact housing. The affordability of a house or apartment and its convenience to work, as well as its comfort and style, will always be factors considered when making decisions about where to live. But what is familiar always enters in, and will have repercussions on what is considered desirable housing in the future. Even in West Van and North Van, where the 2001 census showed a population that is massively native-born and European-descended like Kris and Alex, new influences are being felt. While the census indicated that English was spoken as the home language by more than 90 per cent of the households in both communities, the next most frequently spoken home language was Persian, with Chinese coming not far behind, and both well in advance of Canada's other official language, French. What kind of expectations about cities do newcomers bring? Is the walkable city something they're used to? What is happening to walkability elsewhere in the world as the twenty-first century proceeds?

[CHAPTER 11]

A Quick Turn Around the Block
The Walkable City in Other Parts of the World

FIRST OF ALL, take note: people elsewhere in the world walk a lot more than North Americans do. This is true despite the facts that in European countries the private automobile has long been within reach of ordinary families, and that in some developing nations like China and India a car is becoming a possible dream for millions in the growing middle classes.

In small cities and towns all over the world, however, most people do not have access to a private vehicle. Take, for example, the people walking to work and school on a morning in Lushoto, Tanzania. It will be another month at least before the winter rains begin, and the road is dusty. The sky is gray, however. If we were nearer the coast, the thought might be, "Fog!" But this town, founded when Tanzania was a German colony, lies at 1,417 meters (4,652 feet) altitude and a good 75 kilometers (47 miles) as the crow flies from the sea, so there is no chance that what is obscuring the hills in the distance and the bottom of the valley might condense into precipitation.

No, it is smoke, because the farmers are preparing their patches for planting, burning the debris from the last season, and clearing under-brush that has grown up under the trees in the stand of eucalyptus by the side of the road.

Here, as in many places around the world, people, particularly women, living on the fringes of towns and villages walk immense distances to their fields, to get water, to take their produce to market, and to bring what they buy in town home. One study in Uganda showed that about 75 percent of trips on roads were by foot, 22 percent by bicycle and only 2 percent by vehicle. Another suggested that women were walking an hour each way merely to fetch water in many African villages.

Lushoto, Tanzania. Getting around on foot or bicycle is what most people do most of the time even today.

On this morning, at this hour, no one is walking along the road with a large plastic container of water on her head, however. The foot traffic is mostly children on their way to the school in town, with a few women neatly dressed in brightly-colored kanga wraps carrying things to market. There are a few vehicles on the road; there's a pickup truck ahead of us, and behind us dust swirls up in the air obscuring the truck that is rolling along back there.

As we approach the center of the town, the foot traffic becomes heavier: men in white shirts and dark trousers on their way to work, more children, older women apparently running errands. Near the market square a half dozen buses of various sizes wait to load up with passengers and cargo and head for the surrounding villages or farther away to Moshi, the gateway to Kilimanjaro, or Sone where connections to Tanga on the coast and Dar-es-Salaam are possible.

Lushoto (population 23,256 according to the 2002 census) was built at the beginning of the twentieth century in the West Usambara Mountains as Wilhelmthal, a place where German colonial officials could spend some of the hot, rainy season. Its center is set out on a grid a couple of streets deep like so many colonial towns, but times have changed. Footpaths lead out of town following the contours of the hills, because traffic is nearly all on foot. A four-wheel-drive vehicle may jounce along, stopping to pick up walkers if there is room in the cab or—if it's a truck—in the open back. But the driver and the owner (not necessarily the same person in this country where wages are low) are the big exceptions to the rule. In this part of the world ordinary people walk if they are going under 15 kilometers (about 9 or 10 miles) or so. A trip longer than that is an occasion. A bus ride is something to dress up for.

It's not just in small towns in the developing world that walking is the norm. Take the workers coming back to their barracks from a construction site in the outskirts of the booming mega-city of Shanghai. They are a world away from Lushoto, and the streets they walk down are much broader and better paved than the ones in the West Usambara Mountains. The one thing the hundred or so young Chinese workers have in common with the multi-aged pedestrians going about their business in Lushoto is that they are on foot. According to Shanghai city officials, about 20 per cent of workers walk to their jobs in the Eastern Chinese port city.

Shanghai is currently in the middle of an enormous make-over, designed to insure that 35 percent of its area is "green." Most of this new green space is being created by razing low-rise housing in the center of the city and replacing it with "tower in the park" development, both in the city and also in a broad band of agricultural land around it. While some of the former Puxi (the older section west of the Pu River) residents are able to snare apartments in the new center-city buildings, a sizeable proportion have been lured to the outlying areas of the city by the prospect of two- and three-bedroom apartments. This suburban growth means that getting from home to work may involve commutes as long as those in North American or European suburbs. To improve public transportation, major additions to the subway system are in the works. Some 100 kilometers (about 60 miles) of new line opened in December 2007, completing several loops which make it easier for Shanghai's eighteen million residents to navigate the system. More subway is on the way, so official projections of high commuting by foot are surprising at first glance. But given the fact that many construction and factory sites house their workers (whose permits may only allow limited stays in the city) in nearby barracks, walking to the job is a simple matter for many.

The kind of development going on in Shanghai is only possible where government firmly and effectively holds the levers of power, and can muster the enormous financial resources necessary for massive reconstruction. A similar conjunction of the stars occurred in Haussmann's Paris, but it hasn't happened very often elsewhere.

It is not present in São Paulo, Brazil, which is growing as rapidly as Shanghai, or even more so. Like many other cities in the so-called developing world, São Paulo has a higher density than cities in North America and much of Europe. This is not because of a conscious plan, Enrique Peñalosa, the former mayor of Bogotá, Colombia, notes, but because people in cities like São Paulo and Bogotá must live closer together in order to be near work, given the low level of motorized transport and the lack of highways. All kinds of people walk at least partway to and from work, like those young women swinging down Avenida São Jose in the Centro district about 7 a.m. on a Saturday morning in late summer. There are a half dozen of them, all tall and slim and young and lovely like the girl from Ipanema, although we are a small

Parque Ibirapuera in São Paulo. Walking is frequently faster than car traffic in Brazil's largest city, but the automobile is still the preferred way to get around.

mountain range inland from the sea. They're walking quickly even though they're wearing stiletto high heels. One sings a line from a song, and they all laugh while another does a couple of dance steps.

At first it's a puzzle just where they're going. The only other people out at this hour are the first street sweepers and a tall man in a Rastafarian-like knit cap, leaning against a lamp pole and drinking something from a big paper cup. We cross the empty street—no need to look out for cars now although later on the traffic will fill all lanes—in order to be a little less conspicuous as we follow to see where the young women are going. The shop fronts are closed up, not even one *lanchonete* or café is open for breakfast. The young women cross the main boulevard and cut around a square. They're still walking fast, but the exuberance seems to have been turned down a notch. Then, as a car slows down so the driver can ogle them, it becomes clear what's going on. They're putas, whores, on their way home. Their initial energy was like the whoops kids give when school lets out. Now they have to walk to the buses which will take them to the neighborhoods where they will pass their day, before another night back in the bars of Centro.

The car turns around in the middle of the block and comes back. The driver rolls down the window to talk to the girls. One comes over and leans into the open window. She glances over her shoulder at her friends, who have paused to see what will happen. More talk, more laughter, and the girl opens the door and gets in. The others continue, walking a little faster, but with even less bounce. A ride exchanged for "romance"?

São Paulo, like most of Brazil, is full of privately-owned automobiles. The region is home to Brazil's automobile industry. Until the last fifteen years there has been little investment in subways and light rail, and the traffic jams are legendary. The city even bans cars with odd- or even-numbered license plates on alternate days to cut down on traffic and air pollution. The effect has been minimal, most observers agree, if only because many of those who could, bought another car with a license opposite of the one they already possessed. But it is not only the well-off who have bought into the car culture. Were we to go to any middle- or working-class neighborhood we'd see tiny garages employing no more than two or three men on nearly every street. Watching mechanics at work seems to be as popular a pastime in some neighborhoods as pick-up soccer. Quite clearly many people must walk, but most would prefer not to.

And that of course is a big problem. Cars for everyone is a dream that goes back to Henry Ford who aimed to build automobiles that his workmen could afford. Today as India and China surge forward economically, auto manufacturers in developing countries are moving to meet the latent demand for private cars. In India the Tata Company will soon market its $2,500 U.S. Nano car, as affordable as the Model T and the Volkswagen Bug were in their heydays. While Tata says the new model will be less polluting than the motorbikes and auto rickshaws which now crowd India's streets, the move to private cars bodes ill for the walkability of India's cities. Will there be urban sprawl, or will the increased vehicular traffic simply make it even more dangerous to walk down roads that people must share with cars and trucks?

Only in a few "developing" countries like Singapore has material progress been guided to create a dense, modern, essentially new city where public transportation and foot traffic reign and cars are only tolerated. Late on a hot afternoon near the western end of the island nation, this can be seen at the Pasir Ris subway station and city bus turnaround. It is flooded every couple of minutes as passengers pour out of the subway station to walk home or to catch buses that will take them nearer to their flats. The distances people walk here are never more than three-quarters of a kilometer (half a mile) or so, and as sweat rolls down backs and off foreheads, it's easy to understand why a dense network of buses are desirable. Daytime temperatures stay near 32°C (89.6°F) the year around, and the city-state's first president, Lee Kwan Yew, said that air conditioning is the element which made Singapore's late twentieth-century flowering possible.

Since the mid-1960s Singapore has completely re-housed its citizenry. It was a port city where most people lived crowded together in two-story shop houses or waterfront shanties. Two or more families often shared a room, in conditions that sound like those of Zola's working-class characters in *The Dram Shop*. But a clever plan transformed an existing, British-inspired compulsory retirement savings scheme into a means through which absolutely everyone has a chance to buy an apartment. Capital from the savings plan—currently both employers

Street life in Singapore is vibrant even though it is a city of high-rise housing.

and employees must contribute—was used to build tall apartment towers in "new towns" linked together by good public transportation where people could find work, schools and relatively comfortable places to live. The first units were basic three-room flats available for the poorest and most ill-housed, but in the forty-five years since independence, design and availability have enormously improved. Now 85 percent of Singapore's four million residents live in Housing and Development Board flats, and 90 percent own their own apartment, which may be as large as three bedrooms plus living room and two baths.

Certainly Singapore is far from perfect—its repression of dissidents and punishment for drug offenses are legendary—but it has successfully tackled many of the problems of the walkable city. The benefits are many: little local air pollution, high energy efficiency, water conservation, and high-density neighborhoods where there's still a lively street and community life.

We circle around the park next to the subway station and bus terminus, checking out the playground and the stream which once ran in a concrete culvert but which is being returned to a more natural state with native plants along its banks and birds resting among the bushes. There are lessons here for the rest of the world, and many questions, not the least among them, what should the role of decision-makers in affecting change be. In present day Shanghai and Singapore, as in Haussmann's Paris, the state can play what Jane Jacobs calls a Guardian role, mandating massive change, developing plans and requiring compliance. But the combination of great power and good ideas has not been common over history. Much more common is a patchwork of smaller players and mixed results. In this kind of world, what controls what happens? Who determines the way our cities develop?

Four

Talking the Talk
How to Get There from Here

Chicago's Carson Pirie Scott store designed in 1904 by architect Louis Sullivan who famously said that "Form follows function."

CHAPTER 12

Form Follows Finance, or
Lessons from *Its a Wonderful Life*

Louis Sullivan, the renowned Chicago architect who inspired sky-scraper builders everywhere, famously said, "Form follows function." He was talking about making a new architecture by using techniques perfected at the turn of the twentieth century, such as building with steel framing, and transporting people and goods by elevator. The phrase became a catchword all over the architectural world and throughout the entire century.

Nearly a hundred years later Carol Willis, an architectural critic, took the idea and gave it a twist that resonates even more strongly through discussions of the walkable city: form follows finance. Financial arrangements in the late twentieth century nearly dictated the destruction of the walkable city, and any attempt to rebuild it must rejig economic incentives.

Willis wasn't talking about suburbs and urban renewal in her book *Form Follows Finance: Skyscrapers and Skylines in New York and Chicago*, though. She was examining the way the landscape in which buildings are constructed affects their design, be it the financial landscape or the particular topography of a city. The idea was near-heresy when Willis proposed it. The rest of the world envied and imitated the Manhattan and Chicago skylines. Attempts in post-World War II Paris to transform it into a city of skyscrapers, after all, can be seen as nothing more than lust for buildings that were specifically twentieth-century. Willis's assertion that these signature constructions owe as much to non-design demands as they do architectural genius was extremely provocative.

"Form follows finance" has even larger resonances, however. Singapore's densely populated city of towers in parks is a direct result of the way financial institutions—the compulsory savings scheme and the

Housing and Development Board subsidies for flat-buying—were used. While the desire for a little house on a little bit of land holds a powerful attraction for people all over the world, North America's suburbs would never have developed so extensively if ways had not been found to finance individual houses by the hundreds of thousands.

Before World War II it was extremely difficult for ordinary folk to get together enough money to buy a house. The dream of home ownership lies at the heart of an American classic film, *It's a Wonderful Life*, trotted out every Christmas season because of its feel-good message that one person's small gestures can make a big difference in the world. Jimmy Stewart is George Bailey, and the time the movie was made was immediately after the Second World War. George is ready to end his life because it seems to him that he has done nothing with it and that he has betrayed the folk who had put their money in his family's suddenly cash-strapped building and loan association. His guardian angel, however, shows him what the world would be like if he hadn't been around. He saved his brother's life, stopped an accidental poisoning, rescued his wife from sad and narrow spinsterhood, and, perhaps as importantly, kept the Bailey Building and Loan Association on track as a financial institution helping people realize their dreams of having a home of their own.

The choice of a small, people-centered financial institution as the core of this heart-warming movie seems impossibly old-fashioned these days. During the sub-prime mortgage meltdown of 2007 and 2008, literally millions of families in the United States lost their homes when the financial institutions which held their mortgages foreclosed on them. For the most part they were people just barely making it, people who were simply trying to buy into the American dream. But the financial packages they were sold often came with huge interest rate hikes after a year or so that raised their payments far beyond their ability to pay. Unlike folks who dealt with honest George Bailey's building and loan association, many had been flatly lied to. The fact that they went so far out on a limb reflects both the widespread desire among people to own their own homes and the power that financial institutions wield in molding the cities we live in.

It's a Wonderful Life was made during a time of great relief that the War was over and of great optimism about the future. It also came out just as governments in the United States and Canada were shifting programs of financial aid (particularly mortgage insurance) into high gear. If servicemen and their families had had to depend on building and loans (even benevolent ones like George Bailey's) or on traditional banks, there would never have been the enormous market for housing that developed in the 1950s and 1960s. And if the government lending institutions hadn't set very strict guidelines for what kind of housing would be covered, the landscape created by all those houses might have been quite different. This is the example of form following finance that North Americans born after WWII are most familiar with.

The basic idea behind the government home ownership initiatives was that a federal agency would insist that "approved" lenders offer long-term mortgages to borrowers. The program came with a carrot for the lenders: government-backed mortgage insurance. That meant that in case the homebuyer defaulted, the lender wouldn't be out the money borrowed. Savings and loan associations, like George Bailey's, didn't buy into the plan, but developed a similar one. Started in the 1930s, in part as a spur to housing during a time of great economic distress, the U.S. Federal Housing Administration came into its own after the War. It was joined by the Veteran's Administration loan insurance plan. In Canada the Canada Mortgage and Housing Corporation provided similar encouragement to lending and housing construction. In both countries guidelines mandated such things as what basic services should be provided in a subdivision, what house layouts were preferred, what the setbacks from the street should be, street widths, and building materials. The idea was to guarantee a level of quality that acted as both a protection for the home buyer and a way of weeding out people who were thought likely to default on their loans. Other regulations gave higher weight to developments and neighborhoods that were deemed stable—that is, unlikely to change racially or ethnically. The effect of this was to "red-line" areas, effectively refusing any government-insured housing loans in "risky" neighborhoods. Builders wanting to cash in on the support programs simply didn't build in mixed neighborhoods, or develop subdivisions which would be open to people who weren't white and middle class.

The two sets of strictures—setting physical requirements like minimum lot sizes and investing only in "safe" projects—resulted in the ethnically and racially segregated sprawl that surrounded cities in the U.S. and to a lesser extent in Canada. With rare exceptions the loans were not available for maintenance of existing housing or for multiple dwellings, and these exclusions compounded the problem. Indeed, it could be argued that the mortgage insurance programs had as devastating an effect on the walkability of North American cities as did the advent of the automobile.

But form following finance had another dimension in the mid-twentieth-century United States, one Baron Haussmann would understand. The 1956 Interstate Highway Act in its various manifestations not only financed multi-lane roads between cities and across the country, but also provided a network of roads around and through cities. These served as pathways for development. The road-building meant much demolition of older parts of cities—the fight of Jane Jacobs and her friends against the intrusion of the Lower Manhattan Expressway into Greenwich Village is only one example—and the building of what were essentially escape routes out of the cities. Commuting by automobile became easy, initially at least. In Canada, the programs funding highway construction were somewhat different, but attempts to drive freeways through city centers occurred too, as witness the fight Jacobs and her friends won against the Spadina Expressway that had been proposed in Toronto.

One of the great North American challenges of the next twenty years will be to replace those roads and bridges connecting cities and dividing neighborhoods. Their age—most are approaching the half-century mark—coupled with a couple of decades of penny-pinching by many jurisdictions which under-funded infrastructure upkeep, mean that major maintenance and replacement work is going to have to be done. The collapse of an interstate bridge over the Mississippi in Minneapolis in 2007, as well as that of a highway overpass in Quebec the year before, highlighted the problem.

The response to this situation could be a rethinking of what is needed in the way of highways and roads, and a fundamental re-evaluation of the role of expressways and private vehicles in twenty-first-century cities. More investment in public transit might follow: after all, more buses and light rail would mean fewer cars, with less wear and tear on existing infrastructure. But programs to rebuild roads could turn out to be merely a way of sliding more regional highways into the system which would only make sprawling development easier. In Quebec,

Highways all over North America are going to have to be rebuilt as the infrastructure ages.

for example, the provincial government announced with much flourish that it will invest $1.7 billion in 2008 to repair and replace aging roads. But the plan has been roundly criticized by environ-mentalists because $774 million—about 45 per cent of the total—is earmarked to build new routes around Montreal which they say will only spur urban sprawl.

Many governments with an ideological tilt to the right may use this situation as an excuse to divest the public sector of the responsibility for taking care of roads. For example, look at the debate surrounding the Federal Highway Trust Fund in the U.S. It is supposed to run into financial problems in 2009, even though it is supported by gasoline taxes. The money just isn't there, say some advocates of privatization. Increasing fuel efficiency and a shift toward other fuels mean that gas tax revenues earmarked for roads will decrease, while "public and political support for increasing fuel taxes ... was and continues to be weak," according to the U.S. Department of Transportation Federal Highway Administration's official website. A federal highway funding bill, passed in 2005, was supposed to provide $375 billion for repair and upgrading, but in the end Congress only authorized $286 billion. At the time, the war in Iraq was costing $3 billion a week, which prompted Senator Frank Lautenber, a Democrat from New Jersey, to say that obviously the government was spending a lot of money on other endeavors "that we have to recover and put into our highways."

Already some toll roads in the U.S. have been sold to private enterprises, while Highway 407, a privately financed and privately run toll road around Toronto, has been in existence for several years. Quebec's highway plans include a public-private partnership (PPP) component for the most controversial section, a bridge that will connect an existing expressway to the island of Montreal.

The argument in favor of PPPs turns on the idea that the private sector is supposed to be able to raise capital more easily than governments can, and that they are more likely to "think outside the box." But since their revenue, and eventual profits, come from tolls, they have a vested interest in increasing highway traffic, not decreasing it. Two proposals now being considered in California, for example, involve tunneling under ranges of hills to provide "missing links" in the freeway system whose absence at the moment acts to hinder sprawl. Decisions to go ahead with projects like these will have profound effects on the future of our cities, and while most political jurisdictions require public hearings of some sort before governments undertake PPP agreements, protests have not proved to be very effective in stopping them so far.

As for setting up PPPs to refurbish and maintain existing highways, to date the main interest in the U.S. is in taking over high-traffic roads like the Indiana Turnpike which are essential for industry in a region. Whether aging bridges and overpasses in less crucial areas will interest PPPs is far from certain. The public sector is more likely to be left with the responsibility for less-traveled roads, and will have to pick up the tab for maintenance and replacement without the revenue that might come from tolls on roads ceded to the private sector. So far, though, the idea of simply letting old roads and bridges crumble has been advanced by no one, except oil-crisis critic James Howard Kunstler who says we'll have no choice because we won't have the resources to maintain them. A few voices, on the other hand, have begun talking about seizing this opportunity to rejig the entire relation between city and suburbs by investing in public transportation.

One constant is likely to remain: if there is money to be made from a kind of development, there will be investors interested in getting in on the act. This is particularly true when investment is given substantial tax incentives. A case in point is a nifty little tax-avoiding device called an investment trust. Just how attractive they are for investors can be seen in the way Stephen Harper's Conservative government cracked down on most kinds of investment trusts in 2006. By some estimates the Canadian government stood to lose $1 billion annually in tax revenue if the trend continued because a growing number of corporations, including the telecommunications giant Bell Canada, were reorganizing themselves as these trusts.

However, and very significantly for the future of the development of cities, there was one exemption to the Harper government rules: real estate investment trusts, REITs. They are popular in many industrialized countries. Their form may vary slightly, but the basic idea is the same. A trust—a legal entity which holds money "in trust" for someone—is set up, which then invests the money in real estate of some kind. Then the profits, on which the trust pays no corporate taxes, are distributed to the trust's beneficiaries. Investors run more risk than they would if they put their money in a corporation where liability in case of lawsuits or default is limited, but the returns to trusts are often much greater. Pension funds as well as individuals can buy units in the trust, with the result that REITs provide an enormous pool of capital for real estate development. Westfield, the Australian firm which recently bought Betty York's favorite mall in Carlsbad, was one of the first to take the REIT idea and run with it. The large amount of money it has to invest has "created a huge demand for investment-grade real estate properties like shopping centers." The demand was so big that there weren't enough suitable investment opportunities in Australia, which led to Westfield going international. Its Canadian auxiliary, Artis REIT, now specializes in commercial property in the Western provinces, particularly red-hot Alberta.

Because REITs want to reduce risk, they usually go looking for sure-thing investments, Gary Pivo of the University of Arizona says. This means copying "conventional development" that tends to produce urban sprawl, auto-dependence, and urban decline. His observations are corroborated in a survey done by noted urbanists Joseph E. Gyourko and Witold Rybczynski, which suggests that perceived risk is a roadblock to developing more New Urbanism developments on the outskirts of cities. The survey showed that developers were somewhat favorable to in-fill projects closer to the center of the city, but that overall New Urbanist ideas were considered much riskier than conventional development.

Enter the sub-prime mortgage crisis. Beginning in 2007, it became increasingly clear that a large part of suburban development over the last ten years in the United States was being sold to people who were in over their heads financially, frequently having been lied to by mortgage bankers about just how much they were going to have to pay in the future. As cracks began to show in the financial structure, prices for housing of all sorts began to fall, sending shock waves throughout the financial system. What the fallout for banks and other lending institutions will be over the next few years is far from clear. Nor is it clear what will happen to recently built suburbs where county and municipal governments frequently went out on a financial limb, count-ing on a larger tax base and property tax windfalls to pay for streets, sewer treatment, policing and other services. Foreclosure signs have appeared all over the U.S. and cities are growing worried about what neighborhoods look like when so many houses stand empty. One San Francisco Bay Area bedroom community, Vallejo, declared bankruptcy in May 2008, while Baltimore and Cleveland, both of which had been enjoying a mild center-city upswing, may see ugly, costly urban decay in their closed-in suburbs. And what will happen to the countless families who suddenly see their futures radically different from what they had expected?

It is perhaps a time to remember what the message of *It's a Wonder-ful Life* was. Listen to what one of the characters says to Mr. Potter, the hard-hearted banker whose descendants are the high-finance wizards who've been buying and selling mortgages over the last fifteen years in the U.S., flipping property and leading on people who were only trying to get a little of the dream for themselves:

> "What'd you say just a minute ago? … They had to wait and save their money before they even ought to think of a decent home. Wait! Wait for what? Until their children grow up and leave them? … Do you know how long it takes a working man

to save five thousand dollars? Just remember this, Mr. Potter, that this rabble you're talking about ... they do most of the working and paying and living and dying in this community. Well, is it too much to have them work and pay and live and die in a couple of decent rooms and a bath?"

No, it shouldn't be. But despite some help promised by the U.S. government in the summer of 2008, it may be that North America is going to see families doubling up to pay the rent, couples living in cars, and trouble in general in newly-poor suburbs. Canada, where the sub-prime mortgages are much less common, so far has seen neither massive foreclosures nor plunging real estate prices. But the future looks far from rosy on this, and on several other fronts.

[CHAPTER 13]

The End of the World
in Washington Square

JANE JACOBS' WASHINGTON SQUARE got feature billing in the 2007 futuristic horror film *I Am Legend*. It was not the Washington Square of Henry James or of Jane Jacobs' protests against highway off-ramps and housing destruction, but a Washington Square in the not-to-distant future when a medical experiment gone terribly wrong has killed millions and changed everyone left into monsters.

Everyone, that is, except the star Will Smith who is living with his dog on the Square, holed up in a townhouse where he is working on a way to save what remains of the world. Smith, as Robert Neville, is a scientist who thinks he has found a way to undo the terrible damage wreaked by a virus originally developed as a cancer cure but which has turned into a disaster. Although the film begins with what one critic called "a nifty, wordless car chase," Smith/Neville spends much time walking around the empty, devastated city by day. Buildings are crumbling, lions have escaped from the zoo, cars remain where they were when death overcame their drivers, and at night the dreadful monsters roam, looking for flesh to feast on.

This Washington Square is a universe away not only from that which Henry James and Jane Jacobs knew, but also from the Washington Square where Jane Fonda and Robert Redford romped in the 1967 film *Barefoot in the Park*. That light-hearted comedy poked fun at stuffy middle-class ways, and Fonda and Redford were young and beautiful in it. Since then the world has changed enormously, and so have the two actors. Both became much more politically and socially active as they matured. In 2007, Redford was named one of *Time* magazine's heroes of the environment, honoring nearly four decades of environmental action while Fonda's concern about the safety of nuclear power plants was instrumental in stopping construction of more of them. Behind their actions lies profound disquiet about what we are doing to the world and with scenarios which call for the collapse of society as we know it.

That atmosphere of menace allows *I Am Legend* to produce genuine shivers, even though the premise is far-fetched. Yes, cancers grow when cells quit working the way they ought to. Yes, scientists are using viruses to insert new genes into cells in attempts to control disease. Yes, viral diseases have swept the world in the past. All true, and all cause for reflection, and, possibly, regulation and safeguards.

But no, this is unlikely to be the way the world ends, with the whimper of a German shepherd curled up next to his master. We're far more likely to come to grief because of the way we're living than because of an unstoppable disease that is accidentally let loose. There is no need to go looking for science fiction dangers for shock effect because predictions of the future based in sound research are horrific. The end of oil is just over the horizon, a number of sources assert. Global warming has already doomed the ice cap. Sea levels will rise, the weather will become increasingly violent, croplands will dry out. We may have made an unsustainable mess of this planet. Are we going to reap the whirlwind?

James Howard Kunstler, an admirer of Jane Jacobs, published one of the grimmest warnings for the future in *The Long Emergency: Surviving the Converging Catastrophes of the Twenty-First Century*. His thesis is that for the last 150 years we have been living off the energy from the sun stored over eons. Petroleum is nothing more than the residue of millions of years of sunshine-nurtured plants. Only recently did we learn how to use this immense legacy from deep time to power our machines, move us places, and make things. But this resource is finite. If we have not already used up half of what the past left us, we are nearly there and we certainly have expended that part which is easily harvested. Our current petroleum-powered way of life will be swept away in the turbulence stirred up as the oil runs out. In short, Kunstler says, the end is nigh.

One of the few positive things about Kunstler's analysis is that he says he has no idea just when this end will come. He insists, however, that no energy substitute will take petroleum's place (and certainly the soaring food prices that have recently followed increased use of biofuels suggest great problems even if a substitute turns out to be viable), so we are going to see most things that are powered or made from petroleum disappear or quit functioning, perhaps rather suddenly. The result will be major social dislocation, not the least of which will be in the high-rises of big cities and in their suburbs. People in the former will have no electricity for the elevators necessary in buildings taller than five or six stories, nor will they be able to rely on regular food supplies shipped from agricultural regions often far away. People in the suburbs—"the greatest misallocation of resources in the history of the world," Kunstler says—will have it worse because they will be trapped without fuel for their vehicles. As oil runs out, not only will prices rise, but the uncertainty of supply will destabilize the economic life of the world. He compares what lies before us to the upheavals that followed the Black Plague in fourteenth-century Europe. About the only region of the U.S. that might be able to rebound are the Northeast and upper Midwest where a combination of water resources, farmland, and small towns and cities still retain much of their form developed before petroleum became king, he says.

Concern about possibilities as dreadful as these lies behind *The Walkable City.* One can't ignore dire predictions if one keeps abreast of current events, or drives our roads and sees the soaring price of gasoline. But there is great danger in this kind of apocalyptic thinking. Because we are afraid, we may allow—no, allow is too strong a word because that implies permission and we are not likely to even be informed of what is happening—we may find ourselves deeply involved in scenarios that we would never choose, had we known what the implications were. Using emergencies as excuses, special interest groups and ideologues may grab power and take over resources. Naomi Klein calls this "disaster capitalism" in her muckraking book *The Shock Doctrine.* Free-market economists, inspired by Milton Friedman, Nobel laureate and foremost promoter of the Chicago School of economic thought, use disasters, man-made or natural, as excuses to institute programs and projects that slavishly follow their economic doctrine.

"Only a crisis, actual or perceived, produces real change," Friedman wrote in 1982. "When that crisis occurs, the actions that are taken depend on the ideas that are lying around. That, I believe, is our basic function: to develop alternatives to existing policies, to keep them alive and available until the politically impossible becomes the politically inevitable."

This could be said to have happened in the mid-nineteenth century in Paris, when the perceived problems in the center of the city led to Haussmann's grand plans. Without a doubt, housing was terrible, public health was bad and getting worse, and the streets were overcrowded; something had to be done. Napoléon III came into office with his map of new streets and his vision of a cleaner, healthier, more beautiful city. Haussmann, who had his own ideas of what a great city should encompass, was on hand to direct the work. And behind them both were men of a certain class who saw—as Zola's greedy property developer Saccard does in *The Kill (La Curée)*—a city where "it rains 20-franc gold pieces" on those who guess right about where development will go.

The same sort of perceived threat to the health and well-being of New York was operating when Robert Moses wanted to tear down great swaths of that city to simultaneously get rid of "substandard" housing and to integrate the automobile into the core. The West Village, where Jane Jacobs and her friends'turned back the Moses-led tide, was not nearly as run-down in 1960 as Paris was a hundred years earlier, but the same vocabulary of current disastrous conditions and future dire consequences flowed from the mouths of politicians and their "expert" friends.

Klein says "An atmosphere of panic … frees the hands of politicians to quickly push through radical changes that would otherwise be too unpopular. … In a crisis, debate and democratic process can be handily dismissed as unaffordable luxuries."

Paul Krugman says in his *The Conscience of a Liberal* that over the last thirty years, these same ideas—promoted by what he calls movement conservatives—have increased the gap between rich and poor in the United States, and badly damaged the middle class.

The "emergency" of the U.S.'s war on terror allowed a considerable eroding of civil society; that the Patriot Act allows the U.S. government to check out one's library records is just one of a multitude of infringements on freedoms.

While some of this same war fever has prevailed in Great Britain, Canada has not experienced as much damage to liberties in the interest of conducting a "war." But when it comes to environmental matters, the real problems of supplying energy have allowed a Conservative government to bless massive exploitation of the Alberta oil sands with consequences that are only now becoming apparent. Partly because the projects are so far north of the east-west band of settlement along the Canada-U.S. border where most Canadians live, and partly because many of the people employed by oil sands projects come from regions like Newfoundland which have suffered chronic unemployment, the oil sands didn't receive much scrutiny until recently. Articles in *The New Yorker* by Elizabeth Kolbert in 2007 and a week-long series in *The Globe and Mail* in 2008 explore the high costs of the project, in terms of energy (it takes more than a barrel of extracted petroleum to put two barrels on the market), water, and mutilation of a landscape which will not heal itself for a very long time. It's worth noting in addition that the plight of Newfoundland and Labrador is the result of previous bad calls in managing a crisis. The collapse of the cod stocks on the Grand Banks—once so abundant that France insisted on keeping the fishing islands of Saint-Pierre and Miquelon but gave up the whole of what is now Canada after the British conquest—followed intense commercial over-fishing. "Larger boats and bigger nets were a big investment," Jane Jacobs noted in her book *The Nature of Economies*. "Paying off bigger capital costs added to the pressure to fish diligently." So although some fishery scientists and small-time fisherman saw what was happening and warned against it, they weren't listened to, in a classic "disaster capitalism" worst case.

That's depressing, but on the other hand we must also realize that hardship and danger in the past have sometimes led to projects which improved the lot of ordinary folk. Both Krugman and Klein cite the social programs instituted during the economic depression of the 1930s in many countries as an example of using a crisis to create social programs. These include the great cultural legacy of the Great Depression in the U.S. and Canada when make-work projects sent crews of the unemployed out to work on projects like the botanical gardens in San Francisco and Montreal. In both cases, environmental dreamers had been developing plans for the gardens even though funds for their realization were unavailable. When unemployment relief projects were begun, work could begin right away since the plans were already made: "We started work simultaneously on both ends as well as in the middle," the designer of the Jardin botanique de Montréal, Henry Teuscher, wrote later.

Then came World War II. Income policy instituted at that time, plus the benefits that veterans received in both the U.S. and Canada following the war, combined with programs like American Social Security and Canadian social insurance to create a more than forty-year period when economic inequality declined in both countries. It is a significant accomplishment, Krugman says.

But since the 1970s income gaps have widened in the U.S. as economic policies from Friedman's Chicago School of economic thinking have gained adherents in high places. According to many indicators, inequality in the U.S. is as high was it was during the Depression. The country currently ranks considerably worse than either Canada or the European Union, using an economic index, the Gini coefficient, which compares levels of income across the population: the U.S. measured 45 in 2007, compared to the European Union with 30.7 (2003 estimate), and 32.1 for Canada (2005).

Krugman says it is time to reverse that trend, while Klein notes that conservatives don't have a monopoly on ideas that can be brought into a crisis situation. "Hundreds of thousands of jobs can be created by rebuilding the ailing public infrastructure and making it more friendly to public transit and renewable energy," she writes. "Every crisis is an opportunity; someone will exploit it. The question we face is this: Will the current turmoil become an excuse to transfer yet more public wealth into private hands, to wipe out the last vestiges of the welfare state? … Or will this latest failure of unfettered markets be the catalyst that is needed to revive a spirit of public interest, to get serious about the pressing crises of our time, from gaping inequality to global warming to failing infrastructure?"

"Disaster populism" is needed, Klein says, that is, a response to bad times and disasters that depends on people finding their own solutions to problems instead of being cajoled into acceptance of answers that benefit the big guys. Among the examples she gives of the way this can work are the people in New Orleans who rebuilt on their own after waiting months in vain for help after the Katrina hurricane disaster. What they have accomplished is all the more striking when seen against the background of the way Milton Friedman's principles were used to gut New Orleans's school system in the hurricane's aftermath. Even before the mopping up had really begun Friedman called the disaster "an opportunity to radically reform the education system" in an op-ed piece in *The Wall Street Journal.* He advocated setting up a voucher system and charter schools, and his words did not fall on deaf ears. Two years later, the New Orleans School board which had a 123 schools before Katrina, had only four, while the number of charter schools jumped from seven to 31. There no longer is a teachers' union, because all teachers were fired.

The present-day urban scene is also rife with corollaries of disaster as approvals are wrested from governments to build just about anything that might stimulate business and the economy. A case in point is the current interest in "lifestyle centers," which are little more than imitations of small towns where walking was the main way of getting around. Take, for example, the initial plans to redevelop the historic Griffintown district of Montreal. The center-city neighborhood, already ravaged by industry which tore down factories as it pulled out in the 1960s and 1970s, would be rebuilt to provide housing for fifteen thousand people in a combination of apartment towers, office buildings and retail space. The problem is that the neighborhood is one of the oldest in the city, with a grid street pattern that pre-dates even Manhattan's grand island-wide plan of 1811. It is tightly linked to the St. Lawrence River and the Lachine Canal, where formerly industrial landscapes have been remade into very successful green and recreational spaces. The initial Griffintown redevelopment plans would do away with the closely-grained grid, and replace it with classic tower-in-a-park ideas. Putting aside questions about what a major increase in retail space would do to the city's existing downtown retail sector, the plans would end a very interesting piece-meal redevelopment which has been going on in Griffintown for nearly ten years. There have been a couple of big institutional buildings inserted into the urban fabric—residence halls and classrooms for the technical school of the Université de Québec à Montréal (UQAM) as well as considerable transformation of old factories into loft space for a variety of uses. One building that would be torn down now houses several architects and photographers as well as a restaurant and catering firm. A block away, a store front on the corner is being converted into an art gallery while in the middle of the block an auto-body repair shop stands right beside a shop making custom bicycles. The ensemble is a brilliant example of what Jane Jacobs said happens in mixed-use neighborhoods where low rents help incubate

"Lifestyle centers" are touted as the cure to urban retail ills, but planning agencies can be bulldozed into approving faulty plans for these imitation small town shopping streets. The Quartier Dix30 on Montreal's South Shore is cold and uninviting in winter.

An autobody shop, a gallery on the corner, a small business that makes custom bikes with Montreal's commercial center in the background give a taste of what Griffintown is today. It could be redeveloped a bit at a time in classic Jane Jacobs style as other parts of Montreal like Mile End have been. Or it could be razed and remade in a huge "lifestyle center."

industry and economic vigor. But it looks like the massive development will go ahead, despite much agitation by citizens' groups. Montreal City Council approved revised Griffintown plans in spring 2008, and will even help expropriate property for the project, if necessary.

Devimco, the company behind the Griffintown project, recently built what is supposed to be Canada's first lifestyle center at the intersection of two major freeways on the fringes of suburbia on Montreal's South Shore. The publicity photos for the center (called Quartier Dix30, after the numbers of the nearby freeways) show people lounging around on benches in summer clothes, but for four or five months of the year the center's windswept "main street" seems singularly uninviting. Yet, while thousands of Canadian snowbirds flee the climate when it gets cold, winter does have its special attractions. It is no accident that the unofficial Quebec anthem is a song called "Mon pays, c'est l'hiver"— my country is winter—but Quartier Dix30 seems not to take the region's particularities into account. Critics of the Griffintown project fear that the same insensitivity to what's unusual and interesting will be swept away like *les neiges d'antan*, the snows of yesteryear, in the famous poem by François Villon (who, incidentally, used to while away his time in the cafés of the rue Mouffetard just outside the walls of medieval Paris). Others fear that the first phase of the Griffintown project—the shopping center buildings upon which much of the offices and housing are supposed to be subsequently built—will be the only partially-completed. If economic times turn bad for a long period as petroleum prices rise and the sub-prime mortgage debacle works its way through the economic system, the project could fall under its own weight. Then its walkable city elements—housing near shopping and jobs—would vanish just as definitively as the grid of Griffintown's original streets will as soon as construction begins. And the walkable city, the oldest kind of city, is going to be the key to whatever success we have in meeting the challenges of the future.

In North America there are two paths toward making the best of the situation we find ourselves in. Luckily, that best can be pretty nice, notwithstanding the gloom and doom of prophets like Kunstler, or the horrific vision of an abandoned Manhattan and a Washington Square returned to the laws of the wild in *I Am Legend*. Indeed, the fact that Will Smith is the savior of humanity in that film augurs well for what will happen to us.

[CHAPTER 14]

What We Need on the Journey
How to Avoid the Worst

LET'S LET AL ZELINKA and Hazel Chua show us a couple of paths to solutions.

Hazel Chua, small and dark-haired with sparkly eyes and an infectious laugh, works for Singapore's Housing and Development Board as a public relations officer. She has a vested interest in showing the massive re-housing of Singapore's population over the last forty-five years in the best light. But she's also a young wife, who with her husband has just bought one of the new HDB flats, and is enthusiastically looking forward to decorating it.

They've chosen an upscale flat, classified as four rooms, but containing three bedrooms and a large living-dining area, plus kitchen and bath. They decided not to buy a model with flooring and wall treatments already finished because they can use more of the money they've accumulated in the city-state's compulsory savings plan if they buy it that way. It will be a place to raise a family, perhaps, and certainly an easy place from which to commute.

Hazel leads us around the model apartment—"the show flat"—in the HDB headquarters. It's a bit bigger than the model she and her husband have chosen, with a storage room, and a wall of closets. The furniture is sleek and modern, combining clean lines and bright colors. The windows are masked with curtains and shades, but in a real flat they would all have a grand view of the city, one of the advantages of the way Singapore has adapted the tower-in-the-park idea. Down on the ground, the buildings are surrounded by communal green space, just as Le Corbusier planned, but pedestrian traffic and public transportation take priority over the automobile. From the beginning, Singapore set about to make the island nation easy to get around in by public transportation. Part of the reasoning was based on the need to conserve energy resources, but other benefits have become apparent over the years. Singapore now charges high taxes on private auto sales, and uses electronic tolls to discourage the use of cars.

The HDB flats are available only to Singapore citizens, and immigration control is very strict. Nevertheless, people, often the talented and ambitious, from all over Asia and the Middle East have spent time in the country, working or taking training. Singapore's successes serve as examples of what can be done, while the less successful Le Corbusier-inspired experiments in North America and Europe appear to be forgotten. Like the luxury high-rises going up in Chicago (which have nothing in common with that city's multi-story public housing like the now-razed Robert Taylor Houses except their height), high-rise residential buildings for the wealthier classes have a great deal of cachet in places like Dubai, Shanghai and Mumbai. There is no reason why they can't play a larger role in North America too.

Begun as a way of rehousing the poor, the flats built by the Singapore Housing and Development Board now house more than 85 percent of Singaporeans and come in a wide variety of designs and price ranges.

Jane Jacobs did not have a lot to say about high-rise residential buildings, aside from urging that low-rise buildings not be sacrificed to put them up and to warn that street life may suffer when they are built.

But her beloved Toronto actually has more high-rise residential apartment blocks than any other city in North America besides New York—2,000 compared to the Big Apple's more than 5,000. And even though Toronto's skyline these days is full of cranes building new condo towers, most of the high-rise stock stands in the suburbs and dates from the end of the 1960s. That was the time when the City of Toronto began talking about the problems of suburban sprawl in reaction to the success of Don Mills and its imitators. The region was growing fast, Graeme Stewart writes in an essay on the importance of these buildings to Toronto's future: 30,000 units were built in 1968 alone. "Toronto's use of the concrete high-rise in expanding suburban regions was truly 'smart growth' before the term was coined," Stewart says. The impact has been great on Toronto's ability to run a good transit system. Fewer than 20 percent of renters live in downtown Toronto, with the majority living in the suburbs, fueling demand for public transit without which Toronto would be even more sprawling than it is now.

The first of the apartment towers in West Vancouver dates from about this time too, when a distinctive cluster of tall buildings began to grow up at the end of the Lion's Gate Bridge. Vancouver now comes in fourth in the North American high-rise apartment sweepstakes, after Chicago and before Greater Miami: it has about 600 such buildings, many of them clustered in the city's eminently walkable core. Since the late 1980s, when the former Expo 86 lands were sold to one of Hong Kong's most powerful business interests, apartment towers complemented by a broad range of community services have sprung up. So popular is the whole area with families that a new elementary school was opened in 2004, the first in Vancouver's central districts in more than thirty years. Some of the units have their rents subsidized, but this is not high-rise housing for the poor, which has worked in only a few places, like Singapore.

Toronto's older high-rise buildings were built for middle-class renters. They present some problems today, among them the fact that they leak heat. Built at a time when energy efficiency wasn't a concern, their insulation never was good, and many of them have not had the

Despite its reputation for being a city full of low-rise housing, Toronto has more high-rise residential apartment blocks than any other city in North America besides New York—2,000 compared to the Big Apple's more than 5,000.

best kind of maintenance. Many are separated from each other by fences and roadways which are difficult to cross, so they don't add up to a community the way the new town neighborhoods in Singapore are planned to do. Because of the barriers disturbing the flow of foot traffic, small businesses haven't found the critical mass of passersby necessary to thrive. Residents of the towers often find it easier to get in the car or hop on a bus to buy something than to walk around a set of fences to reach a grocery store that should be only a few minutes walk away, Graeme Stewart says. He proposes setting up programs to encourage retrofitting the buildings to make them more energy-efficient, and permitting more street-level business while looking for ways to integrate buildings into communities.

The shortcomings of Toronto's high-rise housing should not stand in the way of recognizing that the density of population they afford constitutes one of the ways to make cities better places to live. According to Stewart the buildings' defects can be corrected to the benefit of their residents and the city in general. Similarly, the big problem that Kunstler sees in high-rises—the possible lack of electricity to run their elevators— is not enough to remove them from anyone's "to-do" list when thinking about ways to lessen the effect of petroleum shortages. Certainly there is a very good reason why buildings went no taller than five or six stories in Haussmann's day. Before the advent of elevators, to climb higher on a regular basis was more than ordinary folk wanted to do. But there is no reason why solar energy could not be harnessed to power elevators, particularly in places like Singapore where sunshine can be expected twelve hours a day nearly every day of the year. Most tall buildings are already equipped with emergency power sources—generally batteries of some sort—which insure that elevators return to the first floor during an outage. More power batteries could be rigged to provide at least sporadic service during brownouts. Or, were electricity shortages to become regular occurrences, service during mornings and evenings could be assured by the public utility to get people off to work and school, and then back home again at night. The situation is not an all or nothing one, contrary to Kunstler's doomsaying. He expects everything to fall apart at once, seems to dismiss the marvelous resilience of humans, and forgets the rather remarkable record people have had in coping during "emergencies" which sometimes stretch on and on. Just as families in big Indian cities have had to organize their lives around the availability of water from taps that run only a few hours a day, there is no reason to think that people in other parts of the world, even the most pampered, can't figure out ways to cope with periodic problems with elevators. The way that Cuba coped with the sudden withdrawal of foreign exchange and petroleum following the collapse of the Soviet Union is an example of what people can do in hard times. Farming went urban in Havana, with the result that over the last fifteen years the city's gardens have provided an adequate and varied diet for its people.

And the point remains: higher densities through large-scale high-rise development near public transport nodes can go a long way to reducing energy waste that dependence on the individual auto for transportation necessitates, and to setting the scene for a style of living that is more compact, and quite possibly more interesting.

We are stuck, however, with thousands of hectares of suburbs where building whole communities of high-rises is unlikely. What can be done to make them denser and more able to meet the challenges of the future?

Just as apartments are going up in North Van near the SeaBus terminal which takes folks to downtown Vancouver, so some rebuilding is likely to go on near transportation hubs. The Leinberger study of walkable places in the U.S. makes the point that the cities with the most walkable neighborhoods are usually those best served by rail transportation. The existence of rail service (subways, elevated and light rail) in many cases is a legacy from earlier, more compact walkable cities. The harbinger of the future, Leinberger says, is Washington, D.C., with its recently-built subway system around which new walkable development is flourishing. He notes that old rust-belt cities like Detroit and Cleveland have few walkable places, and they may not be able to afford a transition to a new, more compact, walkable plan because of the investment necessary to build modern rail transit systems. Fallout from the sub-prime mortgage mess may make the financial situation of cities like these worse, too, since their property tax revenue is taking a nosedive. This is a shame, Leinberger asserts, because walkable developments in suburban areas elsewhere will be where the action is.

Originally a real estate consultant, Christopher Leinberger's interest in the death of the walkable city in North America is both personal and professional: he grew up loving a small town that had become a suburb of Philadelphia. That childhood had featured the occasional visit to downtown Philly, which he remembers fondly. As a consultant advising investors, he sees walkable, transit-friendly places as good places to make money in future real estate development. The world he pictures is much more cheerful than that which Kunstler sees, but even he has words of caution about what may happen to the suburbs, particularly the far suburbs. Inner suburbs where transit is good may have a much better future, he suggests. Low-density buildings will be torn down and replaced with higher ones as the advantages of living near good transit becomes more evident. But densification is also likely to grow in the quiet, one-house or one-building-at-a-time way that is beginning to happen in Kris Down's North Van neighborhood, just as Jane Jacobs predicted in *Dark Age Ahead.*

Al Zelinka agrees. An urban planner who has thought long and hard about making cities livable, until recently he worked for a firm with offices in the industrial park of one of North America's most famous planned communities. Irvine, California, was designed to mix residential, commercial and industrial space in a harmonious way. Built as an alternative to the creeping suburbanization of Los Angeles, development was initially centered on a new University of California campus, in the 1960s. Now, with most of the land originally scheduled for development built upon, it is home to about 180,000 people with jobs for about a third as many more. There is some bus transport in the area, but nearly everybody who works or lives there uses cars to get from one place to another; the densities may be slightly higher than in ordinary suburbia, but the impact on the use of greenhouse gas-emitting cars and total petroleum use is not that much better.

Until he went to work as planning manager for the nearby city of Fullerton in the summer of 2008, Zelinka's offices were located in a handsome building on a main road in Irvine's industrial and office park area. Mature trees shade the parking lot, and all the nearby buildings are handsomely attuned to the Southern California palette of earth tones, accented by the spectacular flowers of bougainvillea and oleanders. But it's not here that Zelinka thinks the densification necessary to better living will come, but further out in the flat valley of what used to be the Irvine Ranch. That is where the light industry for the planned city is located. Some of the buildings are empty, while others show the signs of only sporadic use: a group of lunch and fast-food places and shops that only have customers for a couple of hours in the middle of the day when workers take a break, for example.

Zelinka says that some of the buildings now zoned for light industry will be transformed into housing the way industrial space in the core of many cities has been gentrified and turned into lofts, boutiques and workshops. Not only would the change bring in higher rents to the owners since the return per square foot for residential space is usually higher than that for industrial space, but it would fill a growing need for affordable housing. Zoning changes most probably would be required, but intelligent planners would not oppose such changes, he says, noting that this transformation is already beginning in the Irvine business complex.

As for his family and himself, Zelinka made a choice some time ago that rhymes a little strangely with the one Kunstler made. The Zelinkas live in the historical heart of Orange, California, once a small regional center in the heart of California's citrus belt. The town was incorporated in 1886, and was linked to the Orange County seat in nearby Santa Ana by horse trolley. The line was eventually acquired by the streetcar and railroad empire of Henry Huntington, who made a fortune on railroad and property development at the end of the nineteenth century. Orange was laid out on a classic grid pattern, with a square in the middle; this Old Town section was included in the National Register of Historic Places in 1997. Most of the structures date from 1888 to 1940; when other California towns were tearing down their old buildings in the post-World War II era, Orange decided to save this heritage of thirteen hundred houses and other buildings, representing fifty different architectural styles.

The lots are narrow, and the streets are laid out for minimal traffic, like those in towns and cities all over North America developed in the same era. Zelinka says he and his family like the mixture of different kinds of people, the easy neighborliness that develops when houses are close together, and the services that are a walk away. The area is a small town that has become engulfed by the spreading suburban metropolis, an island from another time in a sea of twenty-first-century urban sprawl.

Kunstler, in comparison, says he decided to live in a small town in upstate New York about thirty years ago because he liked many of the same sort of things: the way one can walk or bike to the store or bank, the closeness of neighbors, the small town cohesiveness. But instead of being overcome by waves of urbanism, his town was left behind in the backwash of late twentieth-century growth. Farms and factories in the surrounding country fell on bad times and into disrepair. But, he says, when the worst comes (and he expects it, never fear) it will be walkable towns like these that will be able to turn to their own resources to survive and perhaps eventually prosper again.

Orange, California is unlikely to ever be self-sufficient the way it was when thousands and thousands of crates of oranges were shipped out of its railroad station, in the early part of the twentieth century. Nevertheless, the compactness of its Old Town district offers its residents many benefits today, and possibly many more as the petroleum crunch makes itself felt.

Several paths lead to more walkable cities, chief among them densifying existing low-density neighborhoods and building a new brand of tower-in-a-park which may lift its head into the clouds but which never forgets that it is on the ground where people spend most of their time. The rebirth and maintenance of existing walkable areas in cities must be encouraged by what ever means possible. To do otherwise will only aggravate the problems of energy supply and global warming.

In North America we are going to have to live closer together than most of us have been accustomed to. The implications of this major change in how we live will affect all aspects of our lives. Mistrust and fear are the wildcards here. We must pay attention to a number of factors, some of which may seem laughable, but which are important nonetheless.

1. *The need to sweat the small stuff—or not*
Details of living can make the difference between comfortable conditions and ones inspiring rage, rebellion or simple rancor. Whenever people live in close proximity there will be tensions. In her attempt at figuring out how we can get out of our current auto-fueled mess, Jane Jacobs ran down a list of what might arise when industry, entertainment and/ or commercial uses are allowed in residential neighborhoods: noise from mechanical sources; bad smells; air and water pollution; heavy through-traffic or heavy local truck traffic; destruction of the good things in the urban landscape like parks, views, woodlands, sunshine: big signs and intense lights; and what she calls "transgressions against harmonious street scales." The list sounds daunting, but she proposed that all these nuisances could be dealt with by what she called "performance codes" setting acceptable levels. These in essence are regulations, and despite her reputation in some quarters as a libertarian, Jacobs firmly believed that regulations were often necessary, and that violations of them should be dealt with promptly by authorities. As for individuals who transgress, she noted, "People seldom object to unamplified voices in conversation," but do object to "louts in the early morning hours who shout angrily and who urinate on walkways and private property and sick naifs who vomit on walks and gardens …These are best dealt with by police and bar owners." In other words, people ought to respect each other, and when they don't, society's Guardians should act.

Noise is the spoiler of New York, Adam Gopnik says in his book of essays on life in the Big Apple, *Through the Children's Gate*. "Like stories about parking elsewhere in North America, noise stories are everywhere in New York, everyone has them, it is a measure of the down side of living in this vibrant city." Noise signifies "crowding," he writes. "The fight over noise is a displaced fight over space. You struggle so hard to claim a few hundred, a bare thousand, square feet that anything intruding—a take-out menu, a neighbor's piano—becomes an affront to your privacy, to your selfhood." Noise is not small stuff in situations like this, and city officials as well as people who design and build dwellings must be aware of this. Sound-proofing is not a frill, but a necessary condition for decent, compact housing. People who complain about noise are not necessarily cranks, but people trying to make the best of their living conditions.

Another small thing that makes a big difference in compact urban living is access to green. Except where new walkable neighborhoods like Bercy Village in Paris go up in former industrial sites, new large parks are not likely to be part of the densification of cities. Greenbelts surrounding metropolitan areas, established to protect agricultural land, watersheds and natural wonders, may encourage denser development of already-urban places. Like North Van's Grouse Mountain and Hauss-mann's Bois de Boulogne and Bois de Vincennes, they can also provide green destinations for city dwellers in search of wide open spaces not far away. Far more common, however, are chances to insert small squares of greenery and play equipment into the cityscape where a building has been abandoned and reverts to the city for taxes, or where a developer of townhouses is required to deed a small public space to the munici-pality. But that's fine: as Jane Jacobs pointed out, big parks can be scary things if they aren't used or not patrolled. A few benches and some trees in a vest-pocket park just off a shopping street are far more likely to get the regular traffic that insures the informal patrols of "eyes on the streets." Maintenance of street trees, sidewalks planters filled with flowers, zoning flexibility that allows merchants to display flats of plants on the sidewalk and good public transportation to take city center dwellers to large parks on the outskirts are far more effective ways of giving city people close contact with growing things. Community gar-dens, dog walking areas, and friendly competitions for the best garden also help build a community of people who know and look out for each other while enjoying being outside.

On the other hand, being too concerned about another kind of

Small parks and tiny gardens can mean the difference between a dense city that is a pleasure to live in and one that is hot and not.

Dog walkers, like these women in São Paulo, help provide the "eyes on the street" that Jane Jacobs said make neighborhoods safe.

"small stuff", the purity of the cityscape, must be avoided if we are to go on living in evolving cities. No question about it, preserving the details of a fine example of architecture from the past is an admirable goal, but what is more important is the whole urban setting. The kind of redevelopment that went on the Marais section of Paris, where some buildings were modernized so extensively that not much was left but their façades, is not necessarily a bad thing. Minimalist interiors in nineteenth-century New York brownstones or eighteenth-century Paris *hôtels particuliers* may set conservation purists' blood boiling. But no person in the twenty-first century wants to live with old-style plumbing, and a great deal can be said for refitting old buildings for new uses. Jane Jacobs would say they can incubate a multitude of new ideas during the stage when their rents or selling prices are cheap. Even when a neighborhood has been gentrified, with architects coming in to fix up the housing stock, its basic compact street layout remains. Low-rise apartment buildings, attached and semi-detached houses, triplexes (in some places called three-flats) built on smallish lots mean that enough people are going to live in a neighborhood to support a shopping street and public transportation a short walk away. Possibly, even probably, census data will show a small decrease in population per hectare because fewer people will be living in each dwelling after the neighborhood begins to go upscale, but the ratio of dwellings per hectare will not change much. The good points of a compact urban neighborhood will remain, with the added benefits of better sanitation, more fire-resistant materials, and up-to-code electrical wiring.

2. *Taming the walk on the wild side*
A major reason given in the 1960s and '70s for the great move out of the centers of cities in the U.S. was fear. Crime rates were indeed soaring, and a series of riots saw African Americans protesting racial discrimination and lack of civil rights. But walkable neighborhoods were not to blame for that, and indeed some of the worst racial conflict of the period occurred in relatively suburban, auto-dependent neighborhoods, like the Watts section of Los Angeles.

Walkability, Jane Jacobs notes, actually can keep fear at bay. *The Death and Life* is full of stories about the way "eyes on the streets" and a constant stream of foot traffic lessens the opportunity for crime. When people walk along the streets day and night, when houses are close enough together that residents can keep track of what is happening, when people know who belongs in a neighborhood and who is a stranger, it is much harder to get away with wrongdoing. Other researchers since have measured small physical changes that can cut down on crime; a good part of the work that planner Al Zelinka did when he was in private practice was advising cities and developers on such measures. Even such seemingly unrelated matters as allowing people to keep small dogs in apartments have an impact. Dog-walkers go out at all hours of the day and evening, often get to know each other, and constitute an informal neighborhood patrol. Even in cities with very high street crime like São Paulo, Brazil, the presence of women of a certain age promenading their pooches signals that this street at this hour is safe.

Unfortunately, the defaults on suburban mortgages following the sub-prime meltdown are happening largely in suburban neighborhoods that are not dense enough to provide this kind of community control. The crystal meth lab or the marijuana grow-op on that quiet cul-de-sac will go unremarked if the houses around it are empty, while the few neighbors who remain may live in fear. It's worth noting, too, that there has always been rural crime, although popular mythology has down-played it. Canadian crime rates, including murder, are actually higher in villages with populations of less than a thousand than in urban areas of more than 100,000. In the U.S., violent crime rates are still higher in urban areas than in rural ones, but while urban crime has decreased substantially over the last twenty years, decreases in rural rates have not been as rapid. Illicit drug use on the outskirts of town is frequently very high, while lower population density in the country means that law enforcement officers usually have a larger area to patrol than their urban confreres, and, frequently, fewer resources. Talk to farmers whose fields have been taken over by marijuana growers if you want to know what fear is! Unfortunately the enormous number of foreclosures in the newest suburbs of the U.S. will mean declining tax bases for local jurisdictions just at a time when they should be beefing up their police patrols. It's unlikely there will be more funds available to encourage public transportation either, even though residents may find themselves having to commute even farther as they chase a decreasing number of jobs in an economy in trouble. In other words, many North American suburbs may come to resemble the very worst of European suburbs, like those *cités* surrounding Paris which exploded in 2005. As Christopher Leinberger wrote in the March 2008 *Atlantic Monthly*, "fundamental changes in American life may turn today's McMansions into tomorrow's tenements."

Any discussion of fear, however, must recognize the importance of public opinion in stirring things up and creating self-fulfilling prophecies. Television and radio news programming has been based for the last couple of decades on "if it bleeds, it leads," placing much emphasis on the most startling and striking events. As a consequence, fear of crime has risen in the U.S. (and to some extent in Canada) even though crime rates have fallen dramatically since the highs of the 1980s and '90s. Similarly Bernard Marchand attributes middle-class movement out of several suburban *cités* near Paris in the 1990s to fear inflamed by media reports. Surely the media and government have a responsibility not to whip up public opinion or to make political hay out of crime.

3. *Sharing the wealth*

A commitment to decent living standards for everybody through an adequate social safety net, equal opportunity, and good schools is something that every society, rich or poor, should endorse. This doesn't mean that everyone is completely equal economically or that everyone will be rich when the wealth is shared. But inequality makes people in close quarters uncomfortable at the best of times and sabotages society in the worst.

The Guardians—the police, municipal inspectors, the justice system—will find their jobs much easier, and they will be more successful, when conditions of economic equality exist. Adolescents will always do foolhardy things, often dangerous to themselves or others, like the young men racing their cars on the quiet roads near Vellore Park. Other people of all ages have mental or other problems which push them toward antisocial behavior. But where there is relative equality and an expectation of fairness, tensions will be reduced to a minimum "background noise."

For a long period in the middle of the twentieth century, North American countries did a pretty good job of sharing what there was, and because the pot grew bigger during much of the time, ordinary folk saw their lives improve substantially. But, as Krugman points out, that trend reversed in the late 1970s and early 1980s in the United States. Things have not been as bad in Canada; remember, the Gini coefficient of economic inequality still is substantially less than that of the U.S., 32 versus 45. But successive Conservative governments and copycat adoption of American values could undo that. Krugman says that the first step toward renewed equality in the U.S. would be universal health insurance, and the corollary in Canada would be to insure that the health insurance system is not eroded further.

Sharing the wealth should also include ways to help ordinary people acquire homes, be they ever so humble. In North America, aspects of the huge U.S. and Canadian government mortgage insurance programs after World War II can be roundly criticized. Why did they insist on single-family houses in ethnically "pure" neighborhoods, for example? But they bettered the lives of millions of people by giving them the means to acquire adequate housing. The principle of mortgage insurance is not to blame for recent problems with sub-prime mortgages, but relaxing of regulations governing financial institutions is. After the Great Crash of 1929, a system in the U.S. had been set up through which people could save their money in "federally insured deposits in tightly regulated savings banks, and banks used that money to make home loans," Paul Krugman explained in *The New York Times* last spring, when foreclosure rates were spiraling and housing prices had declined all over the U.S. for the thirteenth straight month. "Over time, however, this was partly replaced by a system in which savers put their money in funds that bought asset-backed commercial paper from special investment vehicles that bought collateralized debt obligations created from securitized mortgages—with nary a regulator in sight." The result has been a gathering storm of financial trouble, which may have long-term consequences on the economy all over the world. Yet this should not be used as an excuse to dismiss the widespread desire for good housing that buying sub-prime tapped into. It would be far better to re-regulate the mortgage financing industry and then turn to mechanisms that would help people buy homes, and not necessarily a single-family, edge-of-city place.

Singapore's enforced savings plan has accomplished much, while

La Défense, the large and beautiful office complex outside Paris, was planned with little upscale housing for the people who hold the upscale jobs there. That means that it is usually deserted at night although at noon on a nice day the plazas may be filled with people.

attempts in several developing countries to provide small plots of land on which to build small but sturdy houses are promising. Curitiba, a largish town southeast of São Paulo in Brazil, led the way in the 1990s. When landless families invaded a large area owned but no longer used by railroads, the city took what could have been just another hodge-podge shanty-town development like many seen on the edges of Third World cities, and provided help with land title, mortgages, and house design. The residents of the Bairro Novo (or new neighborhood) built their own houses, usually one room at a time. Along with a deed to the small plot, they also got a fruit tree and an ornamental tree as well as an hour of architect's time to help them plan what they wanted to build. The result: homes for eighty thousand people who are proudly living their dream in far better conditions than they could ever have hoped for if they'd been forced into the settlements of shacks which in Brazil are called *favelas*. Similar initiatives elsewhere include six hundred thousand small housing loans made by the Grameen Bank in Bangladesh and the recognition in many countries that upgrading slums is much, much cheaper than trying to tear them down.

Sharing the wealth in the rest of the world will also require an under-standing by governments, both those receiving and those providing aid, of the importance of distributing the money properly; infrastructure aid should go to help everyone. Klein recounts the example of how aid money in Sri Lanka after the 2004 tsunami went to build the sewers and the water supply necessary for high-end housing and tourist hotels. Obviously, the quality of urban life would be improved by a commitment to the much lower-tech system necessary to make water safe for everyone.

There is a corollary to sharing the wealth: the powerful in the society should be honest and governments should be transparent, however naïve that may sound. In her philosophical musing in *The Systems of Survival*, Jane Jacobs saves her severest criticism for the "monsters" who, she says, arrive when her two systems of social organization, the Guardian and the Traders, are mixed. Certainly she would be appalled at the way the current U.S. government has mixed up its role as Guardian with ideas of Traders in the war in Iraq. Much of this conflict has been outsourced to private companies like Haliburton and Blackwater, with absolutely toxic consequences of lying, blind obedience, cronyism, and enormous hidden waste.

But that needn't be the case. Both Krugman and Klein cite the honesty with which the challenges of both the Great Depression and World War II were met by the administration of Franklin Delano Roosevelt. Government intervention on a scale not previously seen was undertaken with the strictest propriety. Fortunes were made, without a doubt, but the social safety net that was developed during the former and the rationing and fair dealing set up during the latter can serve as examples for today. Kickbacks, side deals, profiteering on construction materials, or building for the sake of making money for cronies should not be tolerated by any government, particularly when substantial changes must be made.

A related problem is the difficulty cities have in finding the mix of housing and jobs that will allow people to live close to where they work. Planners frequently take pains to include industrial parks in their designs for new communities. Don Mills and Vellore Park are cases in point, but the jobs provided don't pay well enough for the job-holders to live in the communities. The reverse is true too: high-end office and research developments are rarely planned today with high-end housing nearby. La Défense outside Paris has been deserted at night and on weekends because its extrodinarily handsome collection of office towers until recently included little upscale housing.

The glory days of Toronto's Annex model, with large, comfortable houses for professionals and academics within walking distance from hospitals and a university campus, are long past. Planners and the public have come to assume that commuting will be necessary for a large proportion of the people who live in any new housing development. Changing this expectation is one of the challenges for coming decades.

4. *Beware of grand projects: what is needed is the human scale*
Let's go back to Paris, imagining what the Baron and Jane Jacobs would see on that spring Sunday afternoon. Were they to make their way to the edge of the Seine, they could lean on a balustrade and look up the dark green water flowing past. The big barges carrying gypsum and gravel are absent for the moment, taking a weekend break perhaps. Tour boats are out, and people from all over the world are craning their necks to see what they can of the white and light-gray city reflecting back the sunlight. Traffic rolls on the boulevards behind the Baron and Ms. Jacobs, but it is lighter than it would be during the week. Part of that is

due to the usual lack of activity on weekends, but part is also the direct result of the current municipal government's plan to give the city back to its citizens.

Lean over the Baron's shoulder and you'll see that the high-speed traffic lanes put in place in the 1960s along the waterfront of the Seine are car-free today. They are not deserted, far from it, but the traffic is on foot and on bicycles. There are people out walking and pushing baby carriages and strollers, young folk on roller blades, elderly couples arm-in-arm, joggers, little kids on tricycle, grownups on bikes.

Ah, yes, bikes. In the spring of 2007 Paris began putting bike rental stands all over the city where for a small fee—the first half-hour is free in fact, once one is signed up—one can rent a bike, ride it for a while and then drop it off. The plan had already proved very successful in Lyon. The hilly terrain there makes biking difficult, but with the drop-off plan riders were able to ride to the edge of the escarpment at the confluence of the Saône and the Rhône, walk down (or up) the hill, and

Paris, which once embraced the automobile, has realized that walkability is important to cities in the twenty-first century. Therefore, the highspeed roadway along the Seine is turned over on Sundays to people who want to walk, pedal, scooter, and skate.

then pick up a bike below or above. Paris is flatter, but skeptics questioned whether the plan would work or whether it would make any difference in either car traffic or congestion on buses and the Métro. The jury is still out on the latter point, but Vélib, with its twenty thousand bikes, has been a resounding success since the beginning. One sees middle-aged men in business suits balancing briefcases on handlebars as they whip through stalled traffic in the center of the city, elegantly dressed women in high-heeled shoes peddling along the *grands boulevards*, young couples on errands passing a fresh baguette between them when paused at traffic lights.

The plan is one of many designed to cut down on car dependency in the city, to decrease automobile traffic by 40 per cent by 2020, compared to figures at the turn of the new century. And unlike London, which has begun heavily taxing vehicular traffic in its historic heart, Paris has chosen not to penalize cars, but to offer alternatives. It has just opened a new light-rail line in the southern part of the city which started carrying about thirty thousand more passengers a day than the fifty thousand expected, even though the trajectory paralleled a successful express bus line. The city is also working with business to cut back truck traffic: Monoprix, which has fifty-six stores in Paris, will soon transport about 40 percent of its stock by train into the city, where it will be transferred to trucks, powered by natural gas, for final delivery.

Paris is not alone in taking measures to make the city more ecologically friendly. Most of the great European cities, including Vienna, Munich, Amsterdam, Barcelona, and Stockholm, have plans to drastically reduce automobile dependency. Their success depends on commitment to good public transportation, and on valuing pre-automobile cityscapes developed when grand projects were conceived on a human scale. In some European cities World War II bombing left great holes in the urban fabric, which have been filled more or less successfully. But modernist attempts to build "twentieth-century" cities, like the skyscraper development south of the Place d'Italie in Paris, were generally less happy additions. In spite of them, the human scale of the cities has remained. Paris is still a compact city where one can walk most places, and if walking is too tiring, public transport is only a few steps away.

***

Just as Toronto city planners in the 1960s, concerned about urban sprawl, encouraged building high-rises in the suburbs, some urban planners have taken a flyer at shaking up car-centric cities. A number of pedestrian mall projects in the 1960s and 1970s were attempts to do just that. Proposed as a way to renew city centers, the idea usually involved tearing down a lot of older buildings to provide parking and barring cars from a stretch of a formerly traffic-clogged downtown street. Sometimes, as in Curitiba as we'll see below, they worked fabulously well, but in North America most were dismal failures. Despite elegant street furniture and active event programming, the malls usually couldn't compete with glittering new shopping centers in the suburbs.

Why? Jane Jacobs would say: because they were boring places that didn't generate enough foot traffic from the immediate neighborhood to keep them safe and lively. The planners' assumption was that shoppers would come to the shopping street by car, so parking had to be provided. Buildings, some of them in poor condition admittedly, would be torn down and at least two or three parking places allotted per 1000 square feet (93 square meters) of retail space. The result was a linear shopping area surrounded by a huge parking no-man's-land, with housing and offices rarely included in the projects. The downtown pedestrian malls were dead after the shops closed because no one had any reason to be there then, and frequently they were dead during business hours too, because not enough business was generated to support an interesting mix of shops.

Contrast this with shopping streets where ordinary foot traffic traveling to and from a combination of shops, housing and workplaces overflows the sidewalks. Turning these streets into pedestrian thorough-fares makes sense. The southern part of rue Mouffetard in Paris is one example, and so is the stretch of Ste-Catherine Street in Montreal which runs through the Gay Village. In both cases, shop owners themselves asked that the street be closed to traffic for part of the day to accom-modate the crowds. But you can't create a real pedestrian mall just by drawing pictures of people on foot and transposing them onto architectural renderings. You need people living in the immediate area to support basic commerce plus easy public transportation to bring people from outside into the neighborhood. The recently developed Bercy Village in Paris is a good example of doing it right: not only does it have a good mix of subsidized, middle-range, and luxury housing immediately surrounding the pedestrian mall, it links easily to Paris's Métro and bus system.

Indeed, public transportation is probably the only kind of grand project that will really work in the future. Subway systems are extremely expensive to build, but may be the only way to provide rapid, comfortable access to a central city without destroying what makes the core worthwhile: its high concentration of people buying, selling, working, living. Light rail systems, particularly outside the core, are beginning to look as attractive as trolleys and tramways once were. Various configurations of bus systems must also be part of the mix.

Translating Haussmann's beautiful boulevards into the twenty-first century is more problematic, however. The temptation for the last fifty years has been to try to adapt them for an automobile-based society. This has meant removing them from contact with the pedestrian, from the context of the walkable city. The beauty of wide thoroughfares and grand vistas is seductive. That certainly seemed the case in the 1970s when Curitiba set out to redo its downtown. This was during a period of dictatorship and the city government had all the powers it needed to tear down buildings to align the main street, as Haussmann had done. The thinking about how cities should be organized had evolved in some quarters, though, and the dictator-appointed mayor and his friends in the city planning department had a different idea. Instead Jaime Lerner, a planner himself, enlisted his staff to convert the street in question into a pedestrian mall in three days. Working frantically over the weekend to put in place a plan which had been discussed and approved but whose implementation the business community had blocked, Lerner's crews tore up pavement, put in benches, and planted flowers along a six-block stretch. When recalcitrant motorists planned a caravan demonstration down the new pedestrian mall a short time later, they were met with a couple of hundred school children sitting on the pavement and drawing pictures in the center of the mall.

The audacious plan worked. Merchants who had been opposed quickly found their business improved and eventually asked for the car-free space to be expanded. (It should be noted that the mall plan did not involve tearing down buildings to make parking: the urban fabric including the basic street layout was not changed, unlike the case of most North American pedestrian mall attempts.) The city under Lerner's leadership went on to become a world leader in transportation, housing, recycling, and other green initiatives. Its integrated system of local and express buses (some of them running every thirty seconds during rush hour) is cited as a way to provide attractive, effective public transportation quickly and at relatively low cost. Lerner retired ten years ago, and has been replaced by city governments which more or less agree with his ideas. While success has brought its own problems—the city's reputation as being a good place to live has attracted hundreds of thousands of new residents, and the transportation system appears to have reached the limit for bus-based transit—Lerner has become the guru of sustainable cities. His worldwide reputation gains him attention for his message.

At the same time, the importance of small efforts, what Naomi Klein would surely call "disaster populism," is getting great press. Lending circles of the kind promoted by Nobel prizewinner Muhammad Yunus and the Grameen Bank appear to be making substantial changes in the way that ordinary people all over the world can finance their small efforts to improve their lot. To listen to Yunus, one can't help be reminded of George Bailey in *It's a Wonderful Life!* People helping people on a small scale can make an enormous difference in how we live. The decisions which each of us make about how and where we live have great repercussions too. The importance of walking, biking, taking public transport, and insisting that our politicians make it easier for us to do so cannot be under-estimated.

So is this a feel-good ending? A vision from an imaginary high point where we can see rough times ahead but the possibility of a resolution where men and women, children and the elderly will be able to live decent lives with enough, if not a lot, and some hope?

Maybe. There is even hope at the heart of one doomsday vision of the future: Will Smith as the hero of *I Am Legend*. Krugman insists in *The Conscience of a Liberal* that anti-African-American racism is the great unmentioned factor distorting politics in the United States. Forces which want to dismantle the societal safety net and which have a great economic interest in rewarding the already well-off have used fear of African-Americans to push forward the policies they favor. But, Krugman says, that appears to be changing. Certainly the strong presidential candidacy of Barack Obama attests to a greater openness among most Americans, but maybe Will Smith playing a role Jimmy Stewart might have been tapped for in another generation says more. Both are decent men doing what they can and in whom we can see our best selves reflected. Only the character Stewart played had a guardian angel on his side. Would that the rest of us had one, too.

[CHAPTER 15]

The House We Bought

ALTHOUGH THE WALK to my husband's office itakes thirty-five minutes, a garage was high on his "must-have" list when we were house-hunting. We both grew up in California, and cars were always part our lives. Unlike our children, who didn't see the point until they were in their mid-twenties, we got our driver's licenses the minute we could. But our car has always spent far more time in the garage than on the road, and in six years our current one has logged merely 24,000 kilometers (nearly 15,000 miles). I would guess that the two of us, taken together, have walked nearly that far.

The high cost of gasoline never entered into our calculations when we were house-hunting, although the oil crunch of 1973, when Middle Eastern oil producers held back production to raise prices, was a recent memory. At the end of the '70s the revolution in Iran had a similar effect. In inflation-adjusted dollars, prices per barrel of oil were moving toward those highs again in 2008; the price was the equivalent of $103.76 U.S. a barrel in 1981, compared to $102.45 U.S. in March 2008. The price at the pump rose a little more quickly: in 2006, gas prices in California surpassed the previous high, the equivalent of $3.27 a gallon recorded in 1981. In between, gas prices everywhere in North America were much lower, so low in fact that 1970s scenes of furious folk waiting in long lines at the gas pump to fill up seem to have faded from the common memory. Certainly the fuel economy measures mandated at the time were long forgotten. More fuel-efficient engines have been transformed into more power, not more miles or kilometer per gallon or liter.

Foolishness, James Howard Kunstler would say, we won't see low prices again. There may be some fluctuations in the price of oil. Part of the 2008 spike in petroleum prices was due to money trying to find a temporary home after being scared out of real estate. But we must

The house the author and her husband bought in the
center of a walkable city.

prepare ourselves for higher and higher prices, and less and less supply, he says. He may be right: the price at the pump in early summer 2008 hit $1.51 CDN a liter (more than $6 CDN per U.S. gallon). That seems enormous, and as I write I note that we haven't taken the car out of the garage for ten days.

But that's the bad news. The good news is that we don't have to.

The legacy of a compact grid street plan plus decent public transportation means that we can get around quite well, thank you very much. Even in the record snows of the winter of 2007-2008, we walked a lot, often arriving faster than buses and cars whose progress was hindered by crazily-parked vehicles and slippery slopes. On the worst days, neighbors broke out cross-country skis and got around central Montreal that way. Deliveries were difficult at times. Tempers flared occasionally. But whereas there were accounts of "snow rage" in suburbs—one senior citizen threatened a snow removal contractor with a shotgun for blowing snow on his lawn—helping dig out the people parked next to you was the behavioral norm in this walkable city.

Perhaps it's exaggerating to ascribe better behavior to walkable city dwellers, but there is one overwhelmingly important point to make about the walkable city: it worked for thousands of years, and there is no reason why it won't work again as we wake up to realize that we should change the way we're living before we are forced to. If we're lucky we may be able to do this calmly, slowly, one block at a time. That would be better than throwing ourselves into a frenzy of activity only to fall back again into an earlier state. Remember that the concern about petroleum resources in the 1970s had absolutely zero effect on the way most North Americans live. If anything, sprawl got worse and vehicles driven got bigger. Nor should we forget the Y2K panic about computers going bonkers at midnight on December 31, 1999. That was a false alarm that at best provided employment for several hundred thousand computer geeks, and at worst teaches that warnings are sometimes much worse than reality.

We bought what in Montreal is called an attached cottage: a two-story row house with cemented basement on a 7.6-by-30.5 meter (25-by-100 foot) lot. When it was built in 1912 by a small contractor it was a short walk from the trolley line leading downtown. Many of the houses on the street have sheltered large families; the family directly across from us bought their house when it was new and raised seven children in it, two of whom were still living there when we arrived. The houses were solidly built to withstand heavy snow loads on flat roofs in the winter, with double windows and skylights whose lower, inner panes opened to allow hot air to escape on summer nights.

We've been happy here. Oh, there was one moment a half dozen years ago when neighbors rushed to put in air conditioners and we seriously thought of moving to some place where we wouldn't be quite so close to machines roaring a couple of meters from our bedroom windows. We went so far as to make an offer on a house with a much bigger garden, but where shops were farther away and public transportation wasn't as good. The offer was turned down in favor of one made a few hours before ours, and afterwards we were glad, so glad in fact, that when the owner contacted us a week later to ask if we were still interested because the first offer had fallen through, our response was an immediate thanks, but no thanks. And, eventually, after a bit of a struggle with local government to get a noise by-law, the worst air-conditioning offenses were brought under control.

At some point, perhaps when our knees give out and we have trouble climbing stairs, we might move to a place on one level. But you can be assured it will be a neighborhood where the world will be waiting outside our door, just a walk away, even if I might have to explore it Jane Jacobs-style, with a walker and an ear trumpet.

Notes on Sources

CHAPTER 1
Looking for a House
Discussion of size of cities comes from a paper presented by Peter Newman at the conference "Australia: Walking the 21st Century," February 20-21, 2001, Perth, Western Australia. Newman notes that Cesare Marchetti developed Marchetti's Constant, which holds that people's average travel time per day is an hour and half. http://www.dpi.wa.gov.au/mediaFiles/ walking_21centconf01keypaper_newman.pdf .

CHAPTER 2
These Feet Were Made for Walking
"Chimpanzee locomotor energetics and the origin of human bipedalism," Sockol, Raichlen and Pontzer. *Proceedings of the National Academy of Science*, July 24, 2007, vol. 104, no. 30, pp. 12265ff. At: http://www.pnas.org/content/104/30/12265.full?sid=d9cb1af2-4d51-46e3-aef2-ca386f9d8d31 .

Speed of humans and other animals:
"Endurance Running and Human Evolution," Bramble and Lieberman. *Nature*, 2004, 432:345.

Bipedal locomotion in animals and skeletal evidence in fossil hominids: For an interesting discussion and photos and diagrams of skeletons and fossils see: http://www.brentrasmussen.com/log/node/54 .

Family with members who walk on all fours:
"A New Syndrome with Quadrupedal Gait, Primitive Speech and Several Mental Retardations: a Live Model for Human Evolution," Uner Tan. *Intern. J. Neuroscience*, 2006, 116, pp. 361ff.

Evidence of shoe-wearing in early humans:
"Early Humans Wore 'Shoes' 30,000 Years Ago." *ScienceDaily*. http://www.sciencedaily.com–/releases/2005/08/050821233037.htm .
"Last Hours of the Ice Man"
http://ngm.nationalgeographic.com/ngm/0707/feature2/
National Geographic series of articles on shoes, print issue September 2006 or http://ngm.nationalgeographic.com/ngm/0609/feature2/index.html .

Speed records for trains:
http://www.spartacus.schoolnet.co.uk/RArainhill.htm .

How far workers would walk:
Unplanned Suburbs: Toronto's American Tragedy 1900 to 1950, Richard Harris. Baltimore and London, Johns Hopkins University Press, 1996.

Walking to go courting:
"Working-Class Isolation and Mobility in Rural Dorset, 1837-1936: A Study of Marriage Distances," P. J. Perry. *Transactions of the Institute of British Geographers*, No. 46, March 1969, p. 121ff. Abstract at http://links.jstor.org/ci?sici=00202754(196903)1%3A46%3C121%3AWIAMIR%3E2.0.CO%3B2-3

Mormon handcart feats:
http://www.uen.org/Lessonplan/preview.cgi?LPid=1279

Gas consumption related to increased weight:
" 'So has their consumption of gasoline,' researchers at the University of Illinois at Urbana-Champaign and Virginia Commonwealth University say," James E. Kloeppel, at:
http://www.news.uiuc.edu/NEWS/06/1024auto.html

CHAPTER 3
The Baron's Paris
The words of Haussmann and Jacobs are their own, taken from their various writings or, in the case of Jacobs, interviews. The Haussmann quotes translated by M. Soderstrom. *Mémoires du Baron Haussmann, Tome II : Grands Travaux de Paris*. Paris, Victor-Havard, 1893. p. 26 ff.

Julien the Apostate on Paris, quoted in *L'Atlas de Paris, Atlas de Paris: Évolution d'un paysage urbain*, Chadych and Leborgne. Paris, Parigramme, 1999 p. 25

Jane Jacobs' comments about Paris:
Interview http://www.kunstler.com/mags_jacobs2.htm
Jane Jacobs interview, Jim Kunstler. *Metropolis Magazine*, March 2001.

Rainy day street scene: *Au bonheur des dames* (*The Ladies' Delight*). Paris, Flammarion, 1999, p. 77. Translation: M. Soderstrom.

"A lady could be quite inconvenienced…" Zola, *La Curée La Curée* (*The Kill*). Paris, Librairie Générale Française, 1996. p. 242. Translation: M. Soderstrom

Haussmann's carriages etc. *Mémoires du Baron Haussmann*, Tome I. Paris, Victor-Havard, 1890. p. 34. Translation: M. Soderstrom.

Origins of people flooding into Paris:
Paris, histoire d'une ville XIe-XX siècle, Bernard Marchand. Paris, Seuil, 1993, p. 20.

"A wistful myth.." Jane Jacobs: *The Death and Life of Great American Cities*. New York, Random House, 1961. p. 4.

Gervaise's impressions of the apartment block., *L'Assommoir* (*The Dram*

Shop). Paris, Flammarion, 2000, p. 66. Translation: M. Soderstrom

"Will it be necessary to let the workers squat without air?" Louis Lazure, Revenue municpale , 10 September 1865, quoted in *Atlas du Paris haussmannien : La ville en héritage du Second Empire à nos jours*, Pierre Pinon. Paris, Parigramme, 2001, p. 92 Translation: M. Soderstrom

"There is no direct, simple relationship between good housing and good behavior. *Death and Life* p. 113.

CHAPTER 4
Jane Jacobs in New York and Toronto
Mannahatta project website:
http://www.wcs.org/sw-high_tech_tools/landscapeecology/mannahatta
"The Mannahatta Project," Nick Paumgarten. *New Yorker*, October 1, 2007, p. 44.

New York population figures:
http://www.demographia.com/db-nyc-ward1800.htm .

"New York is much better shaped for a cucumber than a city," Junius Henry Brown, 1869. In *New York 1880: Architecture and Urbanism in the Gilded Age*, Robert A. M. Stern, Thomas Mellins and David Fisher. New York, Monacelli Press, 1999.

1811 Commissioners' plan for the platting of Manhattan: http://www.library.cornell.edu/Reps/DOCS/nyc1811.htm

"struggling to maintain an honorable independence." *New York 1880*, p. 969.

"..ideal of quiet and of genteel retirement" Henry James, *Washington Square*, p. 16, Penguin Edition, 1963 (first published 1880)

""It's only for three or four years." *Washington Square*, chapter 5.

"Straight gray hair flying every which way":
Jane Kramer. "All the Ranks and Rungs of Mrs. Jacobs' Ladder," *Village Voice*, December 20, 1962, cited in *Ideas that Matter: The Worlds of Jane Jacobs*, ed. by Max Allen, Owen Sound, Ontario, The Ginger Press, 1997.

"I became a good stenographer," from an autobiography Jacobs wrote for *Architect's Journal,* November 22, 1961.

"A Place Called Christopher Street," Jane Jacobs interview with James Howard Kunstler in *Metropolis Magazine*, March 2001.

Population density discussion: *Death and Life*, p. 208. Population density is a slippery concept. Several measures are used: people per acre or hectare, dwellings per acre or hectare, and jobs per acre or hectare. There is the matter of what an acre or a hectare refers to: land surface including streets, residential area including streets or without streets, and so on. When possible dwellings per acre or hectare is used.

Building Dundas and Yonge streets:
John Ross Roberston, *Old Toronto: A Selection of Excerpts from Landmarks of Toronto, edited, integrated and sometimes amended by E. C. Kyte*. Toronto, Macmillan, 1954, p. 130ff.

Question of Separatism, Robin Philpott, "She Stayed Creative till the End:" April 26, 2006, http://www.counterpunch.org/philpot04262006.htmlm In November 2007, former Quebec government delegate to New York Diane Wilhelmy corroborated this role in talking about how Quebec's cultural exports have gone out to conquer markets all over the world. "We trained all these people in the arts—music, theatre, you name it—but of course the market at home is too small to keep them busy. So they had to go elsewhere, which is the origin of the Cirque du Soleil and Robert Lepage's theatrical successes."

Communal meals:
"Dinner with Friends," Gloria Kim. *University of Toronto Magazine*, Spring 2007. At: http://www.magazine.utoronto.ca/07spring/alumninotes.asp

The two systems, Guardian and Trader, are outlined on pp. 23ff of Jane Jacobs, *Systems of Survival: A Dialogue on the Moral Foundations of Commerce and Politics*. New York, Random House, 1992. The 15 characteristic behaviors of each are:

The Trader syndrome:
    Shun force
    Come to voluntary agreements
    Be honest
    Collaborate easily with strangers and aliens
    Compete
    Respect contracts
    Use initiative and enterprise
    Be open to inventiveness and novelty
    Be efficient
    Promote comfort and convenience
    Dissent for the sake of the task
    Invest for productive purposes
    Be industrious
    Be thrifty
    Be optimistic

The Guardian Syndrome:
    Shun trading

Exert prowess
Be obedient and disciplined
Adhere to tradition
Respect hierarchy
Be loyal
Take vengeance
Deceive for the sake of the task
Make rich use of leisure
Be ostentatious
Dispense largesse
Be exclusive
Show fortitude
Be fatalistic
Treasure honor

"When the two systems get confused":
"City Views: Urban Studies Legend Jane Jacobs on Gentrification, the New
Urbanism, and Her Legacy," interview by Bill Steigerwald. *REASON*, June
2001. At: http://reason.com/0106/fe.bs.city.shtml

Jacobs' arrests:
"From Political Outsider to Power Broker in Two Great American Cities:
Jane Jacobs and the Fall of the Urban Renewal Order in New York and
Toronto," Christopher Klemek. *Journal of Urban History*, 2008, 34, p. 309.

CHAPTER 5
Rue Mouffetard, Paris
For a closer look at the Latin Quarter, and for more detailed walks, see *La
Montagne Sainte Geneviève et le Quartier Latin: Guide historique et
architectural*, Alexandre Gady (Paris, Hoêbeke, 1998). The *Atlas de Paris* was
inspirational in writing this chapter.

Origin of Mouffetard:
Paris: The Biography of a City, Colin Jonex. London, Penguin Books, 2004,
p. 203.
Also *The Moveable Feast*, Ernest Hemingway. New York, Scribner, 1964, p. 2.

"Way to hell and gone … where there's always mud up to your knees."
L'Assomoir. The name "Glacière" comes from the ice houses where ice cut
from the ponds of the Bièvre where it spreads out near the Butte aux cailles.
See http://www.bievre.org/ .

CHAPTER 6
Greenland Drive, Toronto
Discussion of zoning as a way of separating different uses in cities:
http://ci.columbia.edu/0240s/0242_2/0242_2_s7_text.html .
Tunnel under Mount Royal:
http://www.railways.incanada.net/candate/tunnel.htm

"Suburban Commuter Rail in Toronto and Montréal," Justin Bur (in 2008, vice president of Transport 2000), April 1984. See: http://www.jbb.poslfit.com/Pages/transportation/1984-04_rail-tor-mtl.html .

"Inspired by Washington, D.C." See: http://www.town.mount-royal.qc.ca/index.php?id=75 .

"Since the end of the last Ice Age":
See: "Ravine City," Chris Hardwicke in *GreenTOpia*. Toronto, House of Anansi, 2007

E. P. Taylor and antecedents of Don Mills:
"Don Mills: E. P. Taylor and Canada's First Corporate Suburb," John Sewell, in *The Second City Book: Studies of Urban and Suburban Canada*, ed. James Lorimer and Evelyn Ross. Toronto, James Lorimer & Company, 1977, p. 18.

"Great Britain put a great deal of emphasis on a fourth possibility: the Garden City":
See: http://www.englishpartnerships.co.uk/newtowns.htm .

Schools in Don Mills:
See school websites at http://www.tdsb.on.ca/ .
The Don Mills Collegiate Institute page includes a charming piece that must have been written in the mid-1970s; Mr. and Mrs. Gerard Lane tell of buying their first house when there were no paved roads and none of the trees which now shade Don Mills streets.

Ann Forsyth on planned unit developments:
"Columbia, Irvine and The Woodlands: Planning Lessons from Three U.S. New Towns of the 1960s and 1970s," Lincoln Institute of Land Policy Working Paper, 2001.

CHAPTER 7
Avenue Vincent-Auriol, Paris: The City After Haussmann
Industrial area in the 13th arronidissement: http://www.technoscience.net/?onglet=glossaire&definition=4100 .

Additional unsuccessful developments in the 13th arrondissement were begun in the 1960s. A huge installation including abbatoirs/meat processing plants was built on the east side of Paris at La Villette to replace the installations at Les Halles. Because of its inadequacies the project was never used. It was destroyed in 1970, shortly after completion. The cost was originally estimated at 174 million francs, but it ended up costing ten times that much, according to Bernard Marchand.

Les Olympiades as the most successful part of the early 13th arrondissement redevelopment:
http://www.insecula.com/salle/MS02699.html .

Red suburbs:
Les Banlieues :Des Singularités françaises aux réalité mondiales, Hervé
Vieillard-Baron. Paris, Hachette Supérieur, 2001, p. 60.
"These apartments worked reasonably well for young families." *Paris,
histoire d'une ville XIX-XX siècle,* p. 285.

Decisiveness of Sarkozy:
"Nicolas Sarkozy sort renforcé de la crise des banlieues" http://
www.lemonde.fr/web/articleinteractif/0,41-0@2-706693,49-710990@51-
704172,0.html

Médine's rap on No. 20, Vincent-Auriol:
http://www.youtube.com/watch?v=wUFIl1iJVBI .

"That … automobile traffic actually declined by 15 percent":
"Paris déclare la guerre aux voitures," Christian Rioux. *Le Devoir,* 14 février
2007.

CHAPTER 8
Vellore Park Road
Diana Birchall, Paul Robinson and Wayne McEachern of the Vaughan
Planning Office, kindly agreed to talk to me; interviews were conducted by
telephone in January and April, 2007 and in person at the town offices in
October, 2007.

"Andrés Duany and Elizabeth Plater-Zybrek looked around": http://
www.slate.com/id/2160718?nav=ais%CE%88 .
"Seaside Revisited, A model town, 25 years later," Witold Rybczynski. *Slate*
online magazine, posted Wednesday, February 28, 2007.

Comments, posted November 9, 2007, on neighborhood website about lack
of walkable shopping:
http://www.cornellvillage.ca/cgibin/yabb/
YaBB.pl?board=CornellRouge;action=display;num=1194651177 .

"The New Urbanists ideas have produced higher densities in Cornell":
"Gross Density and New Urbanism: Comparing Conventional and New
Urbanist Suburbs in Markham, Ontario," Gordon and Vipond. *Journal of
the American Planning Association,* winter 2005, 71/1, pp. 41ff.

"More than 200 randomly selected households":
"New Urbanism and Sprawl: A Toronto Case Study," Andrejs Skaburskis.
Journal of Planning Education and Research 25, pp. 233ff.

"Places to Grow Act": www.elaws.gov.on.ca/html/statutes/english/
elaws_statutes_05p13_e.htm .

"The British had recently been victorious at Vellore":

Vaughan City website: http://www.city.vaughan.on.ca/tourism/history/hisbriefs7.cfm .

Speeding:
http://www.yorkregion.com/News/Thornhill/article/66158 .

Muslim development:
http://www.peacevillage.ca/ .

CHAPTER 9
El Camino Real, Carlsbad California
"As J. Eric Oliver says":
Fat Politics: The Real Story Behind America's Obesity Epidemic, J. Eric Oliver.
New York, Oxford University Press, 2006.

Just how many excess calories are needed for a kilogram of weight gain, or calorie reduction for weight loss, is a topic of great debate among nutritionists. The study "Weight gain and nutritional efficacy in anorexia nervosa" by Dempsey, Crosby, Pertschuk, Feurer, Buzby and Mullen (*American Journal of Clinical Nutrition* 39, pp. 236ff) is frequently cited. Diet counselors use the figure of a pound of body weight equaling 3500 calories. If true, a two-pound weight gain a year translates into only an extra 19 calories a day, which after ten years would mean 20 extra pounds.

"Correlation between urban sprawl and obesity has begun to show up":
"Relationship Between Urban Sprawl and Physical Activity, Obesity, and Morbidity,"
Ewing, Schmid, Killingsworth, Zlot, Raudenbush. *American Journal of Health Promotion* 18/1, September/October 2003.

"The people who choose to live in sprawling neighborhoods may be different from those who don't":
"Fat City: Questioning the Relationship Between Urban Sprawl and Obesity," Eid, Overman, Puga and Turner. Center for Economic Policy Research, March 2007. See: http://www.cepr.org/pubs/new-dps/dplist.asp?dpno=6191 .

"Long Islanders were much less warm to the idea of walking":
"The City Is the Future of the Suburbs, and Other Heresies," Lawrence Downes. *New York Times*, January 29, 2008. http://www.nytimes.com/2008/01/29/opinion/29tue3.html?_r=1&ref=opinion&oref=slogin .

Cuban health during the "Special Period" was also affected by government efforts to keep the country's good health system functioning, and to provide supplementary rations to people at risk such as children, pregnant women and the elderly. See the "Impact of Energy Intake, Physical Activity, and Population-wide Weight Loss on Cardiovascular Disease and Diabetes Mortality in Cuba, 1980–2005," Franco, Ordúñez, Caballero, Tapia.

Granados, Mariana Lazo, José Luís Bernal, Eliseo Guallar and Richard S. Cooper in *American Journal of Epidemiology*, 2007, 166/12, pp. 1374ff at http://aje.oxfordjournals.org/cgi/content/abstract/166/12/1374?ijkey=f5b7c0a6585661c50e6a7774045f4c849bfe2d40&keytype2=tf_ipsecsha

"Canadian statistics suggest that 6,000 deaths a year are caused by air pollution," Joseph Hall. *Toronto Star*, January 29, 2008. See: http://www.thestar.com/living/Health/article/298259 and "Higher Air Pollution Levels Increase Risk for CV Events in Women," Steve Stiles. See: http://www.medscape.com/viewarticle/551686 .

Mall walkers:
Call of the Mall, Paco Underhill. New York, Simon & Schuster, 2004, p. 30.

"By 2007, there were nearly 200 'topless' malls":
"Shoppers turn to town centers," Jayne O'Donnell. *USA TODAY*, January 31, 2007.

CHAPTER 10
Keith Road, North Vancouver, B.C.
North Vancouver before Europeans:
See http://www.joejack.com/coastsalishhistory.html for an interesting overview of Coast Salish customs and history by a Coast Salish artist. Also http://www.leqamellonghouse.ca/about-Leqamel.html .

The origins of places names in North Vancouver have been pieced together from North Vancouver web sites and genealogy sites. In *Namely Vancouver: A Hidden History of Vancouver Place Names* (Vancouver, Arsenal Pulp, 2002) Tom Snyders and Jennifer O'Rourke mistakenly say that Col. Arthur Heywood-Lonsdale was the investor, but he was not born until 1904.

Zoning approvals for densification:
"Duplex Upgrade and Infill, City of North Vancouver" http://www.gvrd.bc.ca/growth/GOMDH2003.htm .

Gas consumption comparisons, Vancouver and Seattle:
Skinny Streets and Green Neighborhoods: Design for Environment and Community, Cynthia Girling and Ronald Kellett. Washington, Island Press, 2005, p. 70.

"17 percent work at home":
Vancouver's Framework for Action: Regional Context Statement www.gvrd.bc.ca/growth/lrsp/rcs/WestVancouverRCS.pd .

It is noteworthy that North Vancouver has won several prizes for its environmental efforts.

CHAPTER 11
A Quick Turn around the Block
Rural women's walking time, adapted from several International Fund for Agricultural Development (IFAD) reports: http://www.ifad.org/gender/learning/role/workload/walkingtime.htm .

Enrique Peñalosa's Lecture "Rethinking Third World Cities Transport," given February 9, 2004 at the conference "Towards more Egalitarian and Sustainable Cities in Developing Countries," Tokyo. He told the *New York Times* in June 2008 that the most important thing that can be done to improve the lot of city-dwellers everywhere in the world is to put in sidewalks. "In developing-world cities, the majority of people don't have cars, so I will say, when you construct a good sidewalk, you are constructing democracy. A sidewalk is a symbol of equality." See "Questions for Enrique Peñalosa, Man with a Plan," Deborah Solomon. *New York Times*, June 8, 2008, at http://www.nytimes.com/2008/06/08/magazine/08WWLN-Q4=t.html?partner=rssnyt&emc=rss .

CHAPTER 12
Form Follows Finance
What Louis Sullivan actually wrote is in an essay entitled "The Tall Office Building Artistically Considered":
> "It is the pervading law of all things organic and inorganic,
> Of all things physical and metaphysical,
> Of all things human and all things super-human,
> Of all true manifestations of the head,
> Of the heart, of the soul,
> That the life is recognizable in its expression,
> That form ever follows function. This is the law."

See: http://www.nga.gov/education/tchan_5_20.shtm.

The copyright on *It's a Wonderful Life* lapsed in 1975, allowing television stations to run it free. But in the 1990s, when Republic Pictures assumed control of the studio which had made the film, it went to court to prove that while the film itself may have gone into the public domain, neither the music nor the original short story on which the film was based on had; now Republic Pictures licenses NBC to show the film twice a year.

Explanation of mortgage insurance:
Creeping Conformity: How Canada Became Suburban 1900-1960, Richard Harris. Toronto, University of Toronto Press, 2004, p. 170.

CHAPTER 13
The End of the World in Washington Square

Time review of *I Am Legend* "Will Smith Gets Lost in His Legend" December 14, 2007 by Richard Corliss http://www.time.com/time/arts/article/0,8599,1694609,00.html?xid=feed-cnn-topics

Robert Redford, hero of the environment http://www.time.com/time/specials/2007/article/0,28804,1663317_1663319_1669890,00.html

"The Jane Fonda Effect" by Stephen J. Dubner and Steven D. Levitt freakonomics.blogs.nytimes.com/2007/09/15/freakonomics-in-the-times-magazine-the-jane-fonda-effect/ September 16, 2007

James Howard Kunstler's evaluation of the state of the world:
The Long Emergency: Surviving the Converging Catastrophes of the Twenty-First Century. New York, Atlantic Monthly Press, 2005.

"Why the Right Loves a Disaster," Naomi Klein. *Los Angeles Times*, January 27, 2008. See: http://www.latimes.com/news/opinion/la-op-naomi27jan27,0,3813752.story .

The Shock Doctrine, Naomi Klein. New York, Metropolitan Books, 2007.

The Conscience of a Liberal, Paul Krugman. New York, W. W. Norton, 2007.

Fishery problems, Jacobs, *The Nature of Economies.* New York, Random House, 2000. p. 97.

"Two gorgeous botanical gardens":
See my *Recreating Eden: A Natural History of Botanical Gardens* (Montreal, Véhicule Press, 2006) for accounts of the way that Eric Walther, Brother Marie-Victorin and Henry Teuscher designed the gardens long before money was committed to the project.

Gini Index:
CIA World Factbook. See:
https://www.cia.gov/library/publications/the-world-factbook/fields/2172.html
and
http://www.energybulletin.net/12271.html .
World statistics show increasing inequity in the world along with increasing social deterioration. Inequity in the U.S. is also increasing, and is at the highest point since the time just before the Great Depression. Inequity was highest during the roaring 1920s and the Great Depression that followed. In the 1930s and '40s, Franklin D. Roosevelt passed laws to make incomes more equal. But from the Reagan era of the 1980s, the trend has reversed. The share of income that goes to the top 5 per cent increased from 16.6 percent in 1970 to 22.4 percent in 2000. In 2001, the amount of income going to the top 20 percent actually passed the 50 percent mark for the first time since the 1930s. In fact, except for the top 20 percent of our population, we are all getting poorer as more and more income shifts to the very top, and the American Dream becomes less and less attainable for more than 80 per cent of the U.S. population.

CHAPTER 14
What We Need on the Journey
Toronto high-rises:
"The Suburban Slab: Retrofitting Our Concrete Legacy for a Sustainable
Future," Graeme Stewart, in *GreenTOpia: Towards a Sustainable Toronto*, ed.
Wilcox, Palassio and Dovercourt. Toronto, Coach House Press, 2007.

Family friendly downtown Vancouver: "Spurring Urban Growth in
Vancouver, One Family at a Time" by Linda Baker, *The New York Times*
December 25, 2005.

Cuba's successful adoption of urban agriculture:
"The good life in Havana: Cuba's green revolution," Andrew Buncombe.
The Independent, at:
http://www.independent.co.uk/news/world/americas/the-good-life-in-
havana-cubas-green-revolution-410930.htmlIndependent.co.uk

How to avoid problems in denser cities. Jane Jacobs, *Dark Age Ahead*. New
York, Random House, 2004. p.156 ff

McMansions into Slums, "The New Slum?" Christopher B. Leinberger.
March 2008 *Atlantic Monthly*.

"Crime rates higher in small cities":
Statistics Canada, June 23,, 2007 at:
http://www.cbc.ca/canada/story/2007/06/28/crime-stats.html . Murder
rates are even higher in rural areas in Canada, which is sharp contrast to the
U.S. where urban rates are twice that of rural rates. Many observers
attribute this to gun control laws. Guns are much less present in Canadian
society.

Rural crime in the U.S.:
http://virtual.clemson.edu/groups/ncrj/rural_crime_facts.htm .

Paul Krugman on the sub prime financial crisis:
http://www.nytimes.com/2008/03/21/opinion/
21krugman.html?scp=3&sq=krugman&st=nyt

Paris bicycles
"20 000 vélos en libre-service vont envahir la capitale française" Christian
Rioux. *Le Devoir*, February 14, 2007.

Curitiba:
"An alternative urban model in Brazil," Bill McKibben, *Mother Jones*,
November 11, 2005 at:
http://www.motherjones.com/commentary/columns/2005/11/curitiba.html

"Recycle City: The Road to Curitiba," Arthur Lubow, *New York Times*, May
20, 2007 at:

http://www.nytimes.com/2007/05/20/magazine/20Curitiba-t.html?pagewanted=6&_r=1&th&emc=th .

Parking spaces per square foot of retail space:
"Shopping Center Parking: How Much Is Enough? " Ralph Bond at: http://www.canadianparking.ca/en/publications/theparker/english_archive/39_SHOPP.PDF .

Boulevard Mont-Royal in Montreal is also poised to become a pedestrian mall for part of the year. It has become a vibrant place in part because of a strategy by a couple of property owners to transform the street from its previous marginal status. Starting by renting to good businesses catering to the daily needs of the surrounding neighborhood like bakeries and fruit and vegetable stores, the owners slowly increased the number of cafés and other food-related businesses before encouraging pharmacies, banks and clothing and shoe shops which attract clients from outside the immediate area. The same thing has been attempted successfully on another Montreal street, Masson, and is being tried in at least three other neighborhoods. See "Nouvelle recette pour revamper la rue principale," François Desjardins, *Le Devoir*, October 7, 2007 at : http://www.ledevoir.com/2007/10/06/159698.html# .

CHAPTER 15
The House We Bought
"Oil Tops Inflation-Adjusted Record Set in 1980," Jad Mouawad at: http://www.nytimes.com/2008/03/04/business/worldbusiness/04oil.html?_r=1&oref=slogin

Historical Yearly Average California Gasoline
Prices per Gallon 1970 to 2007 California Energy Commission
http://www.energy.ca.gov/gasoline/statistics/gasoline_cpi_adjusted.html

Reports by the International Council on Clean Transportation, particularly one on international fuel efficiency standard comparisons: http://www.theicct.org/reports_live.cfm .

Selected Bibliography

BOOKS

Allen, Max, editor. *Ideas that Matter: The Worlds of Jane Jacobs.* Owen Sound, Ont.:The Ginger Press, 1997.

Chadych , Danielle and Dominique Leborgne. *Atlas de Paris Evolution d'un paysage urbain.* Paris: Parigramme, 1999.

Dovercourt, Jonny. Christina Palassio, and Alana Wilcox, editors. *GreenTOpia, Towards a Sustainable Toronto.* Toronto: Coach House Books, 2007.

Gady, Alexandre. *La Montagne Sainte Geneviève et le Quartier Latin: Guide historique et architectural.* Paris: Éditions Hoêbeke, 1998.

Haussmann, Baron Georges-Eugène. *Mémoires du Baron Haussmann, Tome I: Préfecture de la Seine.* Paris: Victor-Havard, Editeur, 1890.

_____. *Mémoires du Baron Haussmann, Tome II: Grands Travaux de Paris.* Paris: Victor-Havard, Editeur 1893.

Harris, Richard. *Unplanned Suburbs: Toronto's American Tragedy 1900 to 1950.* Baltimore and London: The Johns Hopkins University Press, 1996

_____. *Creeping Conformity: How Canada Became Suburban 1900-1960.* Toronto: University of Toronto Press, 2004.

Howard, Ebenezer. *Garden Cities of Tomorrow.* London: Attic Books, re-printed 1985 from 1898 edition.

Jacobs, Jane. *The Death and Life of Great Ameriican Cities.* New York: Random House, 1961.

_____. *The Economy of Cities.* New York: Random House, 1969.

_____. *The Question of Separatism: Quebec and the Struggle over Sovereignty: The Massey Lectures.* New York and Toronto: Random House, 1979.

_____. *Cities and the Wealth of Cities: Principles of Economic Life.* New York: Random House, 1984 .

_____. *Systems of Survival : A Dialogue on the Moral Foundations of Commerce and Politics.* New York: Random House, 1992 .

_____. *The Nature of Economies.* New York: Random House, 2000.

_____. *Dark Age Ahead.* New York: Random House, 2004.

James, Henry. *Washington Square.* London: Penguin Edition, 1963 (first published 1880).

Jones, Colin. *Paris: The Biography of a City.* London: Penguin Books, 2004.

Klein, Naomi. *The Shock Doctrine.* New York: Metropolitan Books, 2007.

Krugman, Paul. *The Conscience of a Liberal.* New York: W. W. Norton. 2007.

Kunstler, James Howard. *The Long Emergency. Surving the Converging Catastrophes of the Twenty-First Century.* New York: Atlantic Monthly Press, 2005.

Lewis, Sinclair. *Main Street*. New York: Signature Classics, 2004.

Mumford, Lewis. *The City in History, It s Origins, Its Transformations, and Its Prospects*. New York: Harcourt, Brace and World, 1961.

Leinberger, Christopher B. *The Option of Urbanism*. Washington: Island Press, 2007.

Lorimer, James and Evelyn Ross, editors. *The Second City Book: Studies of Urban and Suburban Canada*. Toronto: James Lorimer & Company Publishers,1977.

Marchand, Bernard. *Paris, historie d'une ville XIXe-XX siècle*. Paris: Édition du Seuil, 1993.

Mennel, Timothy, Jo Steffens and Chriopher Klemek, editors. *Block by Block: Jane Jacobs and the Future of New York*. Princeton: Princenton Architectural Press, 2007.

Oliver, J. Eric. *Fat Politics: The Real Story Behind America's Obesity Epidemic*. Oxford and New York, Oxford University Press, 2006.

Pinkney, David H. *Napoleon III and the Rebuilding of Paris*. Princeton: Princeton University Press, 1958.

Pinon, Pierre. *Atlas du Paris haussmannien La ville en héritage du Second Empire à nos jours*. Paris: Parigramme 2000

Roberston, John Ross. *Old Toronto: A Selection of Excerpts from Landmarks of Toronto*. Edited, integrated and sometimes amended by E. C. Kyte. Toronto: The Macmillan Company of Cananda, 1954.

Snyders, Tom and Jennifer O'Rourke. *Namely Vancouver: A Hidden History of Vancouver Place Names*, Vancouver, Arsenal Pulp, 2002.

Soderstrom, Mary. *Recreating Eden: A Natural History of Botanical Gardens*. Montreal: Véhicule Press, 2001.

Stern, Robert A.M., Thomas Mellins and David Fisher. *New York 1880: Architecture and Urbanism in the Gilded Age* . New York: The Monacelli Press,1999.

Sutcliffe, Anthony. *The Autumn of Central Paris: The Defeat of Town Planninng 1850-1970*. Montreal: McGill-Queen's University Press, 1971.

Underhill, Paco. *Call of the Mall*. New York: Simon & Schuster, 2004.

Wallace, Alfred Russel, *Darwinism: An Exposition on the Theory of Natural Selection with Some of its Applications*, 1871.

Willis , Carol. *Form Follows Finance: Skyscrapers and Skylines in New York and Chicago*. Princeton: Princeton Architectural Press, 1995.

Vieillard-Baron, Hervé. *Les Banlieues: Des singularités françaises aux réalité mondiales*. Paris: Hachette Supérieur, 2001.

Zola, Émile. *Au bonheur des dames (The Ladies' Delight)*. Paris, Flammarion, 1999.

_____. *L'Assommoir, (The Dram Shop)*. Paris: Flammarion, 2000.

_____. *La Curée (The Kill)*. Paris: Librairie Générale Française, 1996.

ARTICLES

Baker , Linda. "Spurring Urban Growth in Vancouver, One Family at a Time." *The New York Times*, December 25, 2005.

Corliss, Richard. "Will Smith Gets Lost in His Legend." *Time*, December 14, 2007. http://www.time.com/time/arts/article/ 0,8599,1694609,00.html?xid=feed-cnn-topics

Dempsey, D.T., L.O. Crosby, M.J. Pertschuk, I.D. Feurer, G.P. Buzby and J.L. Mullen. "Weight gain and nutritional efficacy in anorexia nervosa." *American Journal of Clinical Nutrition*, Vol 39, 236-242,

Desjardins, François. "Nouvelle recette pour revamper la rue principale." *Le Devoir*, October 7, 2007 at http://www.ledevoir.com/2007/10/06/ 159698.html#w

Downes, Lawrence. "The City Is the Future of the Suburbs, and Other Heresies." *New York Times*, January 29, 2008. http://www.nytimes.com/ 2008/01/29/opinion/29tue3.html?_r=1&ref=opinion&oref=slogin

Eid, Jean, Henry G. Overman, Diego Puga,and Matthew A. Turner. "Fat City: Questioning the Relationship Between Urban Sprawl and Obesity." *Center for Economic Policy Research*, March 2007, http:// www.cepr.org/pubs/new-dps/dplist.asp?dpno=6191

Ewing, Reid, Tom Schmid, Richard Killingsworth, Amy Zlot, Stephen Raudenbush . "Activity, Obesity, and Morbidity" *American Journal of Health Promotion*, September/October 2003, Vol. 18, No. 1

Fantauzzi, Joe. "Senior Charged under Speed Racing Law" York Region News, January 4, 2008 http://www.yorkregion.com/News/Thornhill/ article/66158

Forsyth, Ann. "Columbia, Irvine and The Woodlands: Planning Lessons from Three U.S. New Towns of the 1960s and 1970s." Lincoln Institute of Land Policy Working Paper, April 2001.

Franco, Manuel, and Pedro Orduñez, Benjamín Caballero, José A. Tapia Granados, Mariana Lazo, José Luís Bernal, Eliseo Guallar and Richard S. Cooper. "Impact of Energy Intake, Physical Activity, and Population-wide Weight Loss on Cardiovascular Disease and Diabetes Mortality in Cuba, 1980–2005" in *American Journal of Epidemiology*, 2007 166(12):1374-1380 at http://aje.oxfordjournals.org/cgi/content/abstract/ 166/12/1374?ijkey=f5b7c0a6585661c50e6a7774045f4c849bfe2d40 &keytype2=tf_ipsecsha 0.

Gordon, David and Shayne Vipond. "Gross Density and New Urbanism: Comparing Conventional and New Urbanist Suburbs in Markham, Ontario. *Journal of the American Planning Association*. Winter 2005. Vol. 71, Iss. 1, p. 41-54 (14 pp.)

Gyourko, Joseph E. and Witold Rybczynski. "Financing New Urbanism Projects: Obstacles and Solutions." *Housing Policy Debate* Volume 11, Issue 3, 733.

Hall , Joseph. "Air quality in Ontario: Persistent exposure may be causing cardiac diseases in those with no other risk factors." *Toronto Star Graphic*, January 29, 2008 http://www.thestar.com/living/Health/article/298259

Jacobson, Sheldon H and Laura A, McLay. "Economic Impact of Obestiy on Automobile Fuel Consumption." *The Engineering Economist*, 2006 .

Jones, Carolyn, "Vallejo one of few cities to use Chapter 9." *San Francisco Chronicle*, Sunday, May 11, 2008 See: http://www.sfgate.com/cgi-bin/article.cgi?f=/c/a/2008/05/11/BA6E10JVID.DTL

Kunstler, James Howard. "Jane Jacobs Interviewed" *Metropolis Magazine*, March 2001.

Kerry Gillespie. "4 Milllion More People, But without the Sprawl." *Toronto Star*, June 16, 2006 special section.

Klein, Naomi."Why The Right Loves A Disaster." *Los Angeles Times*, January 27, 2008 www.latimes.com/news/opinion/la-op-naomi27jan27,0,3813752.story

Klemek, Christopher. "From Political Outsider and Power Broker in Two Great American Cities: Jane Jacobs and the Fall of the Urban Renewal Order in New York and Toronto." *Journal of Urban History* 2008; 34; 309.

Krugman, Paul. "Partying Like It's 1929." *New York Times*, March 21, 2008 http://www.nytimes.com/2008/03/21/opinion/21krugman.html?scp=3&sq=krugman&st=nyt

Leinberger, Christopher. "Footloose and Fancy Free: A Field Survey of Walkable Urban Places in the Top 30 U.S. Metropolitan Areas." Washington: Brookings Institution. Fall 2007.

Lehmann-Haupt, Christopher. "An Imaginary Round Table on Social Concerns." February. 18, 1993, *The New York Times* http://query.nytimes.com/gst/fullpage.html?res=9F0CE4D71E31F93BA25751C0A965958260

Lubow, Arthur."Recycle City :The Road to Curitiba." *The New York Times*, May 20, 2007 http://www.nytimes.com/2007/05/20/magazine/20Curitiba-t.html?pagewanted=6&_r=1&th&emc=th

McKibben Bill."An alternative urban model in Brazil" *Mother Jones* November 11, 2005 http://www.motherjones.com/commentary/columns/2005/11/curitiba.html

Micallef, Shawn. "The Good Suburb." *Eye Weekly*, December 05, 2007.

Mouawad, Jad. "Oil Tops Inflation-Adjusted Record Set in 1980." *The New York Time* March 4, 2008. http://www.nytimes.com/2008/03/04/business/worldbusiness/04oil.html?_r=1&oref=

Newman, Peter. "Walking in Historical and International Context—What is the Role of Walking in Cities for 21st Century Economies?" Proceedings of the conference "Australia: Walking the 21st Century," February 21-22, 2001 http:// www.dpi.wa.gov.au/mediaFiles/walking_21centconf01keypaper_newman.pd

O'Donnell, Jayne. "Shoppers Turn to Town Centers" *USA Today*, January 31, 2007 http://www.usatoday.com/money/industries/retail/2007-01-31-anti-mall-usat_x.htm

Paumgarten, Nick. "The Mannahatta Project." *The New Yorker*, October 1, 2007.

Perry, P. J. "Walking to go courting: Working-Class Isolation and Mobility in Rural Dorset, 1837-1936: A Study of Marriage Distance.s" *Transactions of the Institute of British Geographers,* No. 46 (Mar., 1969), pp. 121-141.

Philpott, Robin. "She Stayed Creative till the End." *Counterpunch*, April 26, 2006, http://www.counterpunch.org/philpot04262006.htmlm

Pivo, Gary. "A Call for the Creation of Socially Responsible Real Estate Investment Products." (working paper), November 11, 2004, University of Arizona http://www.u.arizona.edu/~gpivo/

Poole, Robert and Peter Samuel. "The Return of Private Toll Roads." Publication of the United States Department of Transportation—Federal Highway Administration, March/April, 2006, http://www.tfhrc.gov/pubrds/06mar/06.htm

Rioux, Christian. "Paris déclare la guerre aux voitures." *Le Devoir,* February 14, 2007 http:// www.ledevoir.com/2007/02/14/131105.html

Rybczynski , Witold. "Seaside Revisited, A model town, 25 years later." *Slate* February, 28, 2007 http://www.slate.com/id/2160718?nav=ais%CE%88

Skaburskis, Andrejs. "New Urbanism and Sprawl: A Toronto Case Study." *Journal of Planning Education and Research* 25:233-248

Sockol , Michael D., David A. Raichlen, and Herman Pontzer. "Chimpanzee locomotor energetics and the origin of human bipedalism." P*roceedings of the National Academy of Science* , July 24, 2007, vol. 104, no. 30 12265–12269

Solomon, Deborah. "Questions for Enrique Peñalosa, Man with a Plan." *The New York Time s.* June 8, 2008 at http:// www.nytimes.com/2008/06/08/magazine/08WWLN-Q4-t.html?partner=rssnyt&emc=rss

Steigerwald, Bill. "City Views: Urban studies legend Jane Jacobs on gentrification, the New Urbanism, and her legacy," Reason, June 2001.

Stiles, Steve. "Higher Air Pollution Levels Increase Risk for CV Events in Women." *Continuing Medical Education,* February 7, 2007 http://www.medscape.com/viewarticle/551686

Tan, Uner. "A New Syndrome with quadrupedal gait, primitive speech and severl mental retardations a live model for human evolution." *International Journal of Neuroscience*, 116:361–369, 2006

Wolfe, Alan. "How We Live Now." *New York Times*, July 25, 1993http://query.nytimes.com/gst/fullpage.html?res=9F0CE2D61438F936A15754C0A965958260

"Nicolas Sarkozy sort renforcé de la crise des banlieues" http://www.lemonde.fr/ web/articleinteractif/0,41-0@2-706693,49-710990@51-704172,0.html

INTERNET SITES

[Organized by topic alphabetically]

Ecomomic Development and Infrastructure Replacement
Gini Index. CIA World Factbook
https://www.cia.gov/library/publications/the-world-factbook/fields/
2172.html, and
http://www.energybulletin.net/12271.html

"Quebec to pour billions into road, bridge repairs" CBC News, February
    11, 2008
http://www.cbc.ca/canada/montreal/story/2008/02/11/qc-road-work-
plan0211.html -

"U.S. highway system badly in need of repair", report by John W. Schoen
    Monday, June 18, 2007 MSNBC
http://www.msnbc.msn.com/id/20095291/

"Flaherty imposes new tax on income trusts," CBC News, November 1,
    2006
http://www.cbc.ca/money/story/2006/10/31/flaherty.html

Westfield involvement in North American real estate:
http://www.westfieldreit.ca/index.php Artis home bpage.

New York
1811 Commissioners' plan
http://www.library.cornell.edu/Reps/DOCS/nyc1811.htm

Mannahatta project website
http://www.wcs.org/sw-high_tech_tools/landscapeecology/mannahatta

New York population figures (consulted October 3, 2007)
http://www.demographia.com/db-nyc-ward1800.htm

Paris
History of the Bièvre:
http://www.bievre.org/

Industrial area in the 13th arrondissement
http://www.technoscience.net/?onglet=glossaire&definition=4100

Les Olympiades as the most successful part of the early 13th
arrondissement redevelopment
http://www.insecula.com/salle/MS02699.html

Suburbs
Zoning as a way separating different uses in cities:
http://ci.columbia.edu/0240s/0242_2/0242_2_s7_text.html

Tunnel under Mount Royal
http://www.railways.incanada.net/candate/tunnel.htm
http://www.jbb.poslfit.com/Pages/transportation/1984-04_rail-tor-mtl.html

Town of Mount Royal
http://www.town.mount-royal.qc.ca/index.php?id=75

UK Garden Cities;
http://www.englishpartnerships.co.uk/newtowns.htm

"Duplex Upgrade and Infill, City of North Vancouver"
http://www.gvrd.bc.ca/growth/GOMDH2003.htm

North Vancouver before Europeans
http://www.joejack.com/coastsalishhistory.html for an intersting overview
of Coast Salish customs and history by a Coast Salish artist.   0http://
www.leqamellonghouse.ca/about-Leqamel.html

Toronto, Ontario
Schools in Don Mills
http://www.tdsb.on.ca/

Comments on neighborhood website about lack of walkable shopping
http://www.cornellvillage.ca/cgi-bin/yabb/
YaBB.pl?board=CornellRouge;action=display;num=1194651177 post Nov.
9, 2007

Official Vaughan City website
http://www.city.vaughan.on.ca/tourism/history/hisbriefs7.cfm

Muslim development
http://www.peacevillage.ca/

"Places to Grow Act,"
www.elaws.gov.on.ca/html/statutes/english/elaws_statutes_05p13_e.htm

Transportation
"Historical Yearly Average California Gasoline Prices per Gallon 1970 to
    2007," California Energy Commission
http://www.energy.ca.gov/gasoline/statistics/gasoline_cpi_adjusted.html

Reports by the International Council n Clean Transportaion, particularly
    the one international fuel efficiency standard comparisons
http://www.theicct.org/reports_live.cfm

Walking
"Early Humans Wore 'Shoes' 30,000 Years Ago." ScienceDaily. (Retrieved
    January 1, 2008)
http://www.sciencedaily.com– /releases/2005/08/050821233037.htm

Human physiology
 http://www.brentrasmussen.com/log/node/54 April 24, 2007

Mormon handcart feats
http://www.uen.org/Lessonplan/preview.cgi?LPid=1279

National Geographic series on shoes
http://ngm.nationalgeographic.com/ngm/0707/feature2/
http://ngm.nationalgeographic.com/ngm/0609/feature2/index.html
(or the print issue of September 2006.)

Speed records for trains
http://www.spartacus.schoolnet.co.uk/RArainhill.htm

Video
Médine's rap on 20, Vincent-Auriol
http://www.youtube.com/watch?v=wUFIl1iJVBI

"Woodbridge Streetracing"
http://youtube.com/watch?v=jeY4TmI-Mr0&feature=related

Photo Credits

Mary Soderstrom, frontispiece ; *Mémoires du Baron Haussmann*, V. 1 Paris Victor-Havarad, Éditeur 1890, 15 ; Maggie Steber, 16; Arthur Russel Wallace, 20; Leonardo da Vinci, 23; Charles Marville, From *Paris des photographes*, Jean-Claud Gautran, ed., Contrejour Paris, 1989, 33, 45; From *Très Riches Heures: Behind the Gothic Masterpiece* by Lillian Schacherl, (Munich, Prestel, 1997), 39; August Bertsch, from *Paris des photographes*, 40; Eugène Atget, from *Paris des photographes*, 43, 94; From *Paris des photographes*, 45; New York City Commissioners, 57; City Cricket, 63; From *Old Toronto* by John Ross Robertson (Macmillan Co. of Canada, 1954), 69; City of North Vancouver, 155; Singapore Housing and Development Board, 192

All other photographs by Mary Soderstrom.

Acknowledgements

Many thanks are due to Kris Down, Alex Grimble, and Max for their hospitality in North Vancouver, Al Zelinka in Irvine and Hazel Soh Imm Chua in Singapore for the information and observations that they shared with me, David Wylie, Kingsway native, who suggested I check out development north of the Major Mackenzie; Eva Kushner, one of Jane Jacobs' neighbors in Toronto who has allowed us to rent her apartment in Paris several times; Doris Ingerman who showed me New York and Greenwich Village in the hot summer of 1969; the late Betty York, the first mall walker I ever met; Jean-François Guilbault and Bénédicte Magerat who showed us Paris by night and Bercy Village in the afternoon; Adrienne and John Hickman and Cathy Retterer who joined us on our explorations of that great city, and Lee Soderstrom, the best of traveling companions and a great walker.